THIS LITTLE FIRE OF MINE

THIS LITTLE FIRE OF MINE

How Flickers of Doubt Can Spark a Bolder, Brighter Faith

KENDALL MARIAH

NELSON BOOKS
An Imprint of Thomas Nelson

This Little Fire of Mine

Published by Nelson Books, an imprint of Thomas Nelson, 501 Nelson Place, Nashville, TN 37214, USA. Nelson Books and Thomas Nelson are registered trademarks of HarperCollins Christian Publishing, Inc.

The author is represented by Alive Literary Agency, www.aliveliterary.com.

Thomas Nelson titles may be purchased in bulk for educational, business, fundraising, or sales promotional use. For information, please email SpecialMarkets@ThomasNelson.com.

ISBN 978-1-4002-5171-1 (audiobook)
ISBN 978-1-4002-5170-4 (ePub)
ISBN 978-1-4002-5167-4 (TP)

HarperCollins Publishers, Macken House, 39/40 Mayor Street Upper, Dublin 1, D01 C9W8, Ireland (https://www.harpercollins.com)

Library of Congress Cataloging-in-Publication Data

Names: Mariah, Kendall, 1992- author
Title: This little fire of mine : how flickers of doubt can spark a bolder, brighter faith / Kendall Dunn.
Description: Nashville, TN, USA : Nelson Books, [2026] | Summary: "Adoptive mom, Army wife, and influencer Kendall Mariah shows readers that if you are willing to embrace the uncomfortable friction that comes with leaning into big questions and hard conversations, you'll discover a new way to deepen your faith, find your true purpose, and anchor your identity in Christ"-- Provided by publisher.
Identifiers: LCCN 2025037844 (print) | LCCN 2025037845 (ebook) | ISBN 9781400251674 trade paperback | ISBN 9781400251704 ebook
Subjects: LCSH: Faith (Christianity) | Christian life | Mariah, Kendall, 1992-
Classification: LCC BV4637 .M3183 2026 (print) | LCC BV4637 (ebook) LC record available at https://lccn.loc.gov/2025037844
LC ebook record available at https://lccn.loc.gov/2025037845

Art direction: Meg Schmidt
Cover Design: Faceout Studio, Molly von Borstel
Interior Design: Mallory Collins

Printed in the United States of America

25 26 27 28 29 LBC 5 4 3 2 1

CONTENTS

CONTENTS

INTRODUCTION

Feeling the Friction

I WAS ONE OF THOSE LITTLE GIRLS WITH fire in my spirit—the kind of fire that made my Sunday school teachers sigh and exchange knowing glances, the kind that had my mama saying "Lord, help us" every time I opened my mouth. I was bold, unapologetic, and completely unfiltered, asking questions that made grown-ups shift in their seats and offering up my opinions like they were just as good as the preacher's sermon.

When I first learned "This Little Light of Mine," I didn't just sing it—I *believed* it, deep down in my bones. That song wasn't a metaphor to me; it was a marching order. Singing it made me feel bold and confident. I was *not* about to let anyone snuff out my light, and I was sure as heck never going to hide it under a bushel—no, sir. My little light was meant to *shine*, and I figured the brighter, the better.

But somewhere along the way, that fire started to feel like *too much* for the world around me.

I was a high-achieving, gold-star-chasing, rule-following kind of kid, and I learned pretty quickly that people liked me best when I kept my fire controlled—like a decorative scented candle instead of a roaring bonfire, better to be seen than to be felt.

They praised my passion when it was used for the *right* things—leading Bible studies, making straight *A*'s, a reliable Sunday school student, you know, being a good little church girl—but if I ever spoke up in a way that made people uncomfortable, well, that was a different story. I was encouraged—subtly, then not-so-subtly—to soften my edges, to shrink myself just enough so I didn't upset the delicate balance of things. In a strange way, I realized it was okay to lead the boat, but don't dare rock it.

That's when I started to feel it—the internal tingle, the pressure building, manifesting in heat that would crawl up the back of my neck, the tension between what I *should* say and what I *needed* to say. I felt it when I heard things in church that didn't sit right with me but knew I wasn't supposed to question. I felt it when I saw people hurting and wanted to speak up but worried about the consequences. I felt it when I saw "good Christian people" say and do things that didn't line up with the fruit of the Spirit I had learned as a child. I felt it every time I swallowed my words instead of letting them spill out in all their fiery, inconvenient truth.

I started calling it *soul friction*.

Soul friction is that holy discomfort—the uneasiness that settles in your spirit when you know something isn't right but aren't sure what to do about it. It's that season of wrestling, where you have more questions than answers, where the things you thought were set in stone start to shift beneath your feet. It's the moment when your tidy, black-and-white understanding of the world is suddenly splashed with color, and you realize that maybe things aren't as simple as you once believed. You realize that the world can no longer be simply categorized, and you begin to uncover nuance and discover shifts of perspectives.

And let me tell you—when soul friction sets in, you *feel* it.

It can be frustrating, unsettling, even painful at times. It can feel like your stomach has flipped upside down, because what do you mean, *I could be wrong? I didn't see the whole picture or know the whole truth?*

But I've come to believe soul friction is one of the most important parts of spiritual growth. Because if we never let ourselves wrestle, never let ourselves question, never let ourselves feel the heat of that friction, how do we ever expect to be refined? Renewed? Redeemed?

INTRODUCTION

We all experience soul friction. It's a sign that we're growing, that we're engaging with the world in a way that forces us to wrestle and reckon with what we thought we knew. We live in a time when information is everywhere, where stories collide, and where perspectives challenge us. Staying in an echo chamber is impossible unless we choose to put our heads in the sand.

And when that friction comes knocking? It's a choice. You can ignore it. Pretend you didn't hear it. Push it down and keep quiet.

Or you can let it guide you. It's not always earth-shattering moments; sometimes it's little moments and questions that add up like sparks turning into a flame and starting a fire.

There is a choice you have to make: Are you going to let that fire burn it all down? Or do you want to let that flame help refine and cultivate a bolder and brighter faith? This book is about the fire inside us—the one that soul friction and discomfort spark.

In part 1, we'll talk about how soul friction and doubt can be a guiding light. It's not always a bad thing. It makes us sit up, pay attention, and strengthen our faith.

In part 2, I'll share the times when soul friction shaped me the most, the moments that changed everything for me. I'll ask you to wrestle with some of the same inconsistencies that I faced and encourage you to pursue a life that's whole and honest—where your insides match your outsides and your words reflect the full truth.

In part 3, I'll guide you through formative questions and help you take a spiritual inventory of yourself and your faith. We'll get deep and be honest about how we really feel and what we actually believe.

I wrote this book because I want you to learn how to trust your soul friction—that little tingle in your spirit, that slow burn in your chest, that unsettled feeling that whispers, *Something about this isn't sitting right*. I want you to stop brushing it off, stop second-guessing yourself, and stop shrinking back just because it would be easier and make others more comfortable to stay quiet.

See, I spent too many years trying to ignore that friction. I'd feel it stir inside me when someone said something that didn't line up with the Jesus I knew—the one who sat with the outcasts, who defended the broken, who flipped tables when the religious folks put power over people. I'd feel it when I saw good-hearted people getting pushed to the margins, when I heard truth twisted into something cold and condemning, when I knew deep down that love was being used as a weapon instead of a refuge.

But instead of trusting that friction, I swallowed it. I pushed it down, told myself I was imagining things, convinced myself that rocking the boat would only make things worse. I believed the lie of *Who would listen to me anyway?* I thought maybe if I just prayed more, stayed in my lane, and focused on my own little corner of the world, the tension in my spirit would go away.

But that's not how it works; soul friction doesn't just disappear. No, friend, it lingers. It simmers. It refuses to be ignored. And eventually, if you let it, it does something miraculous.

It leads you.

Because that friction? That holy discomfort? That's the Spirit nudging you toward something deeper—toward a richer faith that isn't afraid of hard questions, toward a love that is wider and wilder than you ever imagined, toward a courage that doesn't just sit still but *moves* in the direction of truth.

I want you to trust that friction, not fear it.

I want you to lean in when something stirs in your soul, to listen when your spirit is unsettled, to ask the hard questions even when you don't know where they'll lead. Because I believe with everything in me that when you do, you won't lose your faith—you'll find a deeper, truer version of it. One that is built not on fear but on fire. One that doesn't just settle for comfort but seeks out *truth*. One that looks a whole lot less like blind certainty and a whole lot more like *bold love*.

And isn't that what we're called to, after all?

So if you've ever felt that friction—the kind that makes your stomach twist and your heart race and your palms sweat—I hope this book helps you see it for what it is. Not a burden, not a sign that you're doing something wrong, but a *guide*. A spark. A flame inside you that is ready to burn bright and light the way forward.

Because if we don't carry the fire, if we don't tend to it and keep it burning—who else will?

part one

A GUIDING LIGHT

FIRE IS BOTH FIERCE AND PURIFYING, A force that consumes but also transforms. It refines by burning away the excess, stripping down what is unnecessary until only the strongest, truest parts remain. Gold is refined in fire—not to destroy it but to make it purer, more valuable. And faith, much like gold, is strengthened in the heat of trials.

When we walk through seasons of hardship, uncertainty, and suffering, the fire may feel unbearable, but it is not without purpose. It reveals what we truly believe, forcing us to let go of what was never meant to last and cling tightly to what is eternal. Fire doesn't just test—it *transforms*. It turns raw, unshaped material into something strong, something enduring, something beautiful.

And in the same way, faith forged in the fire doesn't come out weaker—it comes out refined, resilient, and radiant, a testimony to what has been endured and overcome.

In this first section of the book, I want to challenge the idea that questions are dangerous and that doubt equals a crisis of faith. Instead, I want to propose that those moments of friction—the ones that make us squirm—can actually be used to strengthen and deepen our personal practice of faith.

Have you ever watched the show *How It's Made*—you know, the one where they walk you through how everyday things are created and manufactured? It's one of those shows I'll throw on as background noise, or if I see it on the TV guide in a hotel room, I don't search any further. I love the concept of discovering how something came to be. I want to understand the creative process, the strategic purpose, and the logistics behind all these random objects.

I know I can't be the only one who likes this show. A show doesn't rack up 312 episodes in this day and age unless there are a whole lot of people just as curious as me. I think we're wired to be naturally curious. And that curiosity doesn't stop at wanting to know how kayaks are made or how wind turbines get assembled—like we see on the show.

Maybe *How It's Made* isn't your cup of tea, but

maybe you're a researcher by nature. You're the friend or the spouse who *lives* to plan the next trip, because you get a thrill out of digging into new places to visit, foods to try, and experiences to chase.

Or maybe you're that parent who immediately downloaded every baby development app the second your child was born. You knew more about sleep cycles, wake windows, and feeding patterns than you ever imagined you'd care about, but you dove in headfirst, determined to get to the root of questions like *Why is my baby crying at 2:00 a.m. even after she's been fed, burped, changed, and snuggled?*

That kind of curiosity often starts with something simple—a question:

- I wonder how that's made?
- Where's the best place to travel in your thirties?
- Why does my baby hate the car but love her car seat? (A personal one of mine.)

Questions are a good thing. But somewhere along the way, they got a bad rap in the church and in Christian culture. When those questions go unanswered and start swirling around in our heads, they can become the start of what I call "soul friction."

For some odd reason, asking questions—especially

the "how" and "why" of our faith—got labeled as a sign of weak belief. And once you start asking those questions, it's a slippery slope to doubt, and heaven forbid a good Christian have any doubts . . . right?

One

WHEN FRICTION BECOMES FIRE

THAT CHILLY JANUARY MORNING MIGHT HAVE looked normal to the outside world. Just another daybreak, the sky barely blushing awake, the hum of neighbors starting their routines, the distant rattle of garbage trucks lumbering down the street. But inside our little home, nothing about it felt normal at all.

I had dressed with intention. I was really trying to lean in to the phrase my mom used to repeat to me while getting ready in the morning before high school: "Look good, feel good, do good." If today was going to suck, at least we were going to look good while it did. My hair was curled, my makeup was set just right, not because I was trying to impress anyone but because I needed something—anything—that I could control. So, I slipped into my signature look: SPANX leggings that held me together in more ways than one, a crisp button-down that made me feel just a little bit put-together, and my trusty slide-on flats that had walked me through seasons of waiting before. It was the kind of outfit that said *I've got this*, even if I wasn't sure I did. Even if the only thing holding me up was sheer willpower and a strong cup of coffee.

Zadie Ann, my tiny five-week-old miracle, was dressed like a little Southern doll: soft-pink smocked dress with lace details, tights covering her tiny legs. I had smoothed her hair, kissed her round cheeks, and tucked a blanket around her, as if wrapping her up tight could shield her from the weight of the morning. She had no idea that today was different. No idea that her daddy was about to get on a plane and leave for months. No idea that the three of us would walk out of this house together but only two of us would come back.

While I packed the diaper bag, double-checking everything even though I'd already triple-checked, Justin was outside, loading his army bags into the car. The sound of zippers, of buckles snapping into place, of gear shifting—it was a soundtrack I knew too well. The steady rhythm of a life dictated by deployments and trainings, where goodbyes were rehearsed and see-you-laters were second nature.

I had spent the night before having my "good cry." The kind where I didn't just tear up but *broke down*, letting it all out in the dark while Justin held me. It was the only safe space to fall apart before I had to pull myself back together. I had allowed myself to feel it all: the frustration of an untimely deployment, the exhaustion of new motherhood, the deep, aching question that sat heavy in my chest: "How am I going to do this by myself?"

I had whispered it into his shoulder, my voice small, shaky. Not because I doubted my love for our daughter but because I had never pictured *this*—learning how to be a mom while also learning how to do it alone.

Justin had held me tight, his voice steady, his words an anchor. "You will be fine. You were made for this."

And he was right. I knew I could do it. I knew I *would* do it. I had spent my life preparing for things I didn't see coming, adapting, pivoting, holding things together when life threatened to pull them apart. I was built for resilience. And this wasn't my first rodeo with separation. I had sent Justin off before, had watched him disappear into a crowd of camouflage, had counted the days until he came back.

But this time, the weight of it felt different.

Six months ago we weren't even in the adoption process. We weren't picking out names, decorating a nursery, or imagining late-night feedings. And yet, here

I was, holding our daughter—the answer to so many prayers—while also preparing to say "See you later" to my husband.

A blessing and a heartache. Tangled together. A friction.

It felt cruel and beautiful at the same time. Like life had handed me my biggest joy and my hardest goodbye in the same breath.

I stood in the doorway, watching as Justin adjusted his gear, his face calm, practiced. He had done this before. So had I. But never quite like this.

And then, the moment came.

The kind of moment that seems to stretch out longer than it should, where every little detail gets seared into memory—the smell of his aftershave and hair pomade, the way his boots thudded against the pavement, the way Zadie Ann's tiny fingers curled into my sweater as if she could feel the shift in the air.

If I opened my mouth, I knew the dam would break. I had been holding it together all morning, willing myself to be strong, to be steady, to not crumble into a mess of tears in the middle of this parking lot.

But he knew. He could feel it in the way I clung to him, in the way my breath hitched against his shoulder. "Look at me." His voice was gentle but firm, coaxing me out of my silence. I lifted my chin, my eyes glassy but locked on his. "Kendall, I love you, and it will all be okay. You *can* handle it."

I nodded, my lips pressed together, still refusing to let a single tear escape. If I started crying now, I might not stop.

We hugged one last time. He kissed me, then kissed the top of Zadie Ann's head, his hand lingering just a little longer than usual.

And then he was gone.

I stood watching as he walked away and joined his soldiers, the lump in my throat growing by the second. Zadie Ann slept peacefully in her car seat, unaware of the moment that had just split our world in two.

The silence that followed was heavy. But there we were. And ready or not, the day had come.

Justin is the best "boy scout" to never actually be a Boy Scout. Need Neosporin? He's got it. In a perfectly organized pouch next to some Tylenol, a few Band-Aids, and—because he thinks of *everything*—a travel pack of Clorox wipes. Need a comb? He's got one tucked inside his wallet, just in case. He even carries a lighter, despite the fact that he hasn't smoked cigarettes in over fifteen years.

It's who he is—prepared, steady, a walking emergency kit with a heart of gold.

And those qualities? They're two of the things I love most about him. His ability to think ahead, to anticipate a problem before it even happens, to be *ready* for anything—it's what makes me feel safe. What makes me feel like I can take a deep breath and exhale, because if Justin's around, it's going to be okay.

Which is probably why I was already spiraling, wondering *how* I was supposed to function without him at home.

See, I'm not exactly what you'd call a *planner.* I am a beautiful mess, a walking contradiction of high ambition and lost car keys, someone who can pull off a major project with tenacity and excellence but also forget where I set my coffee three minutes ago and struggle to keep my room in order. My neurodivergent brain was not gifted with the ability to judge time, to filter my thoughts before they come spilling out, or to execute the simplest of tasks without somehow tripping over something along the way.

We are opposites in the truest sense of the word. But it's the kind of friction that works—the kind that smooths out the rough edges, that makes life richer and more whole.

And the thought of doing it all without him? Without that steady presence, without the person who remembers things when I forget, who grounds me when I spiral, who has been my safe place since I was fifteen years old? That part I wasn't ready for.

I had been saying "See you later" to this boy since he went away to college. We had spent more years apart than together, navigating long distances, late-night phone calls, and countdown apps on our phones. I had been through this before.

But this time, it was different. This time, he wasn't just leaving *me*. This time, there was a tiny baby girl, completely unaware that today was her very first "see you later." The first of many, but that didn't make it any easier.

The day wasn't over, and as much as I wanted to go home, crawl into bed, and lose myself in a Nicholas Sparks movie—something predictable, something where I already knew the ending—I couldn't.

Because life keeps moving. Because *I* had to keep moving.

So I got to work. I reached for the pre-measured formula and the warm water I had stashed in my Yeti, mixing it with hands that were still trembling slightly but growing steadier with each second. Zadie Ann latched onto the bottle, her little hands resting against mine, completely content in that moment. She didn't know her world had shifted that day. She didn't know how much had just changed.

But I did.

I watched her drink, repeating the words in my head like a mantra. *I can do this. I can totally do this.* And maybe, just maybe, if I said it enough, it would become true.

I laid Zadie Ann in her bassinet, watching the way her tiny chest rose and fell in steady little breaths, completely unbothered by the weight of the day. And I thought about what Justin had said. *It will be okay. You can handle it.*

And you know what? He was right. I would be fine. I would figure it out. I would learn, slowly but surely, that missing him and moving forward weren't mutually exclusive.

That I could love him and long for him and still thrive.

That I could wish he was home and still be happy.

That both things could be true.

FRICTION CAN REFINE YOU

Friction is created by the movement of two opposing forces—an uncomfortable rubbing that grates, grinds, and ultimately *changes* whatever it touches. It's not a passive thing. It sparks. It stirs. And if you let it, it can set something ablaze.

That fire can bring warmth, casting light into dark places and igniting something within us that we didn't even know was there. But fire doesn't just illuminate—it refines. It exposes. And, if left unchecked, it can consume and destroy.

For me, this concept of *soul friction* lives in those moments of *uncomfortable juxtaposition*—the places where two things that *shouldn't coexist* somehow do. Where heartache collides with blessing. Where joy sneaks its way into grief. Where deep sorrow walks hand in hand with gratitude.

It's in those spaces that friction does its work.

Sometimes friction shows up like a gentle warmth—the glow of revelation, the spark of passion, the kind of refining that softens rough edges and makes us better.

But sometimes friction isn't warm and fuzzy. Sometimes it's sharp and searing. Because sometimes, friction *hurts*. It rubs against the tender parts of our lives, the places we'd rather keep protected. It exposes what we don't want to see. It makes us face the truth that life doesn't always unfold the way we imagined, that hardship is not a matter of *if* but *when*.

Those hard seasons? They're the friction that wears away our illusions, that scrapes off the filters we've carefully placed over our lives and confronts us with reality. And reality isn't always easy to swallow.

Friction shows up in grief over a prayer that never got answered.

It shows up in loss, in loneliness, in diagnoses that come out of nowhere.

It shows up in uncertainty—the kind that keeps you awake at night, wondering if the job will last, if the money will stretch, if the people you love will stay.

It shows up in the deep ache for stability in a world that seems anything *but* stable.

And when we're standing in that place of pain and confusion, everything in our flesh tells us, *It's not supposed to be like this.* So, we react. We scramble to make sense of it, to assign blame, to find someone—*anyone*—to hold responsible. *If this is happening, then someone must have messed up.* And when we can't find a person to blame, we turn our frustration toward the heavens.

This is not good. So, God must not be good.

But here's the thing about friction: It's not just about pain. It's about *transformation.*

Yes, it can burn. Yes, it can be uncomfortable. But it also has the power to change us—to shape us, to strengthen us, to make us into something we never would have become if we had only ever lived in ease and comfort.

We don't have to face hardship as victims. We don't have to let it define us, or break us, or convince us that we are helpless in the fire. Because while friction may feel like destruction, it can also be *refinement.* And what comes out on the other side? That's where the real fire begins.

FIRE CAN TRANSFORM YOU

These seasons of friction—these moments of tension, hardship, and uncertainty—could have been the things that held me back. They could have paralyzed me, convinced me to stay stuck, to react out of fear, to let my circumstances define me. But instead, I have learned to let them become *catalysts*—not roadblocks but *fuel* that moves my life forward.

Because here's the thing: We don't have to be passive participants in our own story. Life will hand us valleys. That's a given. At some point or another, we will all find ourselves deep in the pit—whether it's heartbreak, loss, disappointment, or the kind of waiting that makes us wonder if God even remembers our name. And when we're there, it's easy to believe that this is it. That the valley is the final destination. That the pit is where the story ends.

But if there's one thing I have learned, it's this: The pit is exactly where God specializes in showing up. Not in the polished, picture-perfect moments. Not when everything is going smoothly. But in the *mess*, in the *wreckage*, in the middle of the place you swore you'd never end up.

And somehow, even there, even in the hardest seasons, there are still moments to celebrate.

Maybe it's a small, unexpected joy that finds its way

into a dark day. Maybe it's the right person showing up at just the right time. Maybe it's the quiet whisper of peace that settles in when you least expect it.

That's what friction does. It challenges us, but it also *transforms* us. It forces us to dig deeper, to build a more resilient faith, to stop waiting for perfect circumstances and start *believing* that even in the tension, even in the unanswered prayers, even in the middle of the valley, there is *still* goodness to be found.

Because the pit? It's not the ending. It's just the place where the real work begins, and just two and a half months into that deployment I got a crash course.

I had finally started to hit my stride as a solo parent. Well, mostly. It wasn't always graceful—more like a controlled stumble—but I was making it work, just like my husband had assured me I would. Turns out, necessity really *is* the mother of invention. For instance, did you know that "Circle of Life" from *The Lion King* is four minutes and six seconds long? And did you also know that, under the right circumstances—namely, desperation and sheer survival mode—you *can* take a full shower in that amount of time?

I certainly didn't.

Not until I discovered that the *only* thing capable of holding my newborn's attention long enough for me to step away from her was a high-definition, animal-stampede-filled musical masterpiece. Who knew baby entertainment and personal hygiene could go hand in hand? I sure didn't, but there I was, lathering shampoo at the speed of light while Zadie Ann stared, wide-eyed, at the TV, utterly mesmerized by Mufasa's grand introduction.

Then there was my other great revelation: relocating the Baby Keurig, aka the Baby Brezza, to the bedroom. Why, you ask? Because I am simply *not* built to stumble through a dark house at 2:00 a.m., fumbling with bottles like a contestant on some high-stakes reality show. No, ma'am. If I could roll over, press a button, and have a perfectly warm bottle ready without even leaving my bed, then I was *absolutely* going to make that happen. Lazy or genius? I'll let you decide, but I know which side I'm on.

The point is, I was *killing it*.

Not only had I figured out the day-to-day logistics of taking care of an infant solo, but I had also cracked the code on *traveling* with one. Since Justin's deployment was noncombat, we were able to visit him, and before she even hit three months old, my tiny road warrior had already taken ten plane rides like a seasoned traveler.

Zadie Ann was an *airplane pro*: bottle at takeoff, nap at cruising altitude, a little charm for the flight attendants, and boom, we were at our destination. Meanwhile, I had mastered the fine art of navigating security lines, juggling carry-ons, and bouncing a baby through the terminal without breaking a sweat, or at least without *looking* like I was breaking a sweat.

So, yeah.

Was it chaotic? Absolutely.

Was I exhausted? Without a doubt.

But was I doing it? Oh, you *bet* I was.

But my stride came to a screeching halt in March—right along with the rest of the world.

One minute I was conquering solo parenting, juggling bottles and flights and midnight feedings like a pro. The next I was clutching my phone, scrolling through headlines, and trying to make sense of words like *quarantine* and *social distancing* that had suddenly hijacked the English language.

"What is coronavirus?"

"Can you get corona from a gas pump?"

"Where can I buy toilet paper?"

"How do you sew a mask?"

These were the deeply intellectual, slightly panicked questions I found myself frantically googling in those early days of lockdown. I had a newborn. My husband was gone. My closest family member was five hundred miles away. And suddenly the world outside my front door felt more dangerous than it ever had before.

So I stayed put. For *five weeks* I never left the house. *Not once*. The only person I saw in that time was my assistant/friend Brigette. We swore to see only each other, and she was just as nervous about this new normal as I was.

I became an expert at grocery delivery, rationed my last roll of toilet paper like it was gold, and honed my at-home self-tan routine to a level of near perfection. My days were filled with an endless rotation of diaper changes, bottle washing, and the occasional binge-watch of *Tiger King*—because, like the rest of America, I needed *something* to distract me from the chaos.

And when that wasn't enough, I did what any sleep-deprived, socially starved millennial mom would do: I downloaded TikTok. What else was I supposed to do? I didn't even have another adult to talk to in person. And let's be honest, you can only FaceTime your mom so many times in one day before she starts hitting you with "Okay, honey, I really should get some things done."

So I made videos. Silly little ones, mostly to entertain myself. And somehow, in between the isolation and the uncertainty, I found moments of levity. But just when I thought I was getting a handle on this whole *pandemic + solo parenting* equation, life flipped the script again.

A little over a month into the lockdown, it was time for Zadie Ann's four-month well-baby checkup. And let me tell you, I was not prepared. Remember, I hadn't left my house in a *month*. I was the *definition* of a paranoid first-time mom, the kind who Lysol'd Amazon packages and side-eyed anyone who so much as cleared their throat.

And now I had to take my baby *out into the world*. A world that suddenly felt like a science experiment gone wrong. A world where invisible germs lurked on every surface, where six feet of distance was the new social contract, where people hoarded Clorox wipes like they were currency.

I wasn't just nervous. I was terrified. And yet, there was no avoiding it.

So, armed with hand sanitizer, a freshly washed car seat cover, and more anxiety than I knew what to do with, I took a deep breath and stepped out into the unknown.

We made it out the door and to the parking lot of the pediatrician's office, where we sat in the car, waiting to be called in. I was jittery but eager—excited to see how much Zadie Ann had grown, but also just *so ready* for some interaction with another adult who wasn't on the other end of a screen.

The appointment started out completely normal. No red flags.

The doctor was warm and reassuring, taking her time with us. She asked how I was adjusting—first-time mom, husband deployed, middle of a global pandemic. She didn't rush through it. She let me talk. I appreciated that.

And then came the usual "Do you have any concerns?"

I hesitated. "Well, actually . . . I don't think it's anything too major," I said, "but I've noticed that Zadie Ann's right nostril doesn't seem to be open all the way. I've been taking photos to track it, and it looks like the opening is getting smaller."

I expected a casual "Oh, that's normal" or "Let me take a quick look and we'll keep an eye on it."

But that's not what happened. Instead, her head tilted ever so slightly. A flicker of something unreadable crossed her face.

"Can I see the photos?"

I pulled out my phone and handed it over, and that's when her expression shifted. She grabbed her flashlight and leaned in closer, inspecting Zadie Ann's tiny nose with an intensity that made my stomach twist. I could see it in her eyes—her *wheels were turning*, her calm exterior giving way to something much more serious.

Then, without a word, she excused herself.

I knew.

I knew.

I didn't have a single piece of medical training, but I *knew* she wasn't coming back into that room to tell me everything was fine. My gut screamed it.

The seconds stretched unbearably as I sat there, holding my baby close, my heartbeat drumming against my ribs. When the doctor finally came back, her face said everything before she even opened her mouth. Her eyes were screaming *red alert*.

My heart dropped like a stone, a sickening free fall into my stomach.

"I think you need to go to Vanderbilt Children's Hospital," she said carefully. "I believe there's a mass in Zadie Ann's face. I'm concerned about it constricting her airway and it could be attached to her brain."

I felt my breath hitch. A *mass on her brain*? Constricting her *airway*?

She continued, her voice steady but urgent. "Because of the lockdown, Vanderbilt isn't taking new appointments. So you'll need to go through the emergency room."

The emergency room. I sat there, frozen for a moment, her words echoing inside my skull. An hour ago I was worried about wiping down the exam table with a Clorox wipe. Now I was being told my baby might have a mass blocking her airway.

A pit opened in my stomach, and for the first time in my life, I felt something I can describe only as *primal fear*.

This wasn't just *friction*. This was *fire*.

I could have thrown up right there in the pediatrician's office. My stomach twisted, my vision blurred, and my breath felt too shallow, too fast.

I had just seen the news. Hospitals were admitting only COVID-19 patients, life-threatening emergencies, and critical procedures. This wasn't something routine, like getting her tonsils removed. This was something else entirely.

The whole drive to Vanderbilt, I yelled at God. This time, the friction wasn't just inside me—it was between my faith and the brutal reality in front of me. How could God *let this happen*? Didn't he see what I was already carrying? Wasn't it enough that I was parenting alone, that Justin was gone, that the world was shut down?

Forty-eight hours later, I was still asking the same questions, only now I was alone in the silent hallways of Vanderbilt Children's Hospital, watching as they wheeled my baby into the operating room.

I had been told to prepare to meet with a team of doctors, an oncologist, a neurologist, and a plastic surgeon. The mass could be *cancerous*. It could be *attached to her brain*.

And because of the lockdown, my mom couldn't come inside to be with me. She had risked all the germs of flying and made the trip, but she couldn't come any closer than the hospital garage. Justin couldn't get on a plane home. It was just me.

The gravity of it all settled on my chest like a weight I couldn't shake. The waiting room was eerily quiet. I counted three mothers, including myself. One waiting for her child's *brain surgery*. Another for *heart surgery*.

I paced. I prayed. I begged God to *do something.* Then I went numb. At some point, my body just shut off the ability to cry. I went into autopilot, watching the clock, gripping my phone, feeling the longest hour of my life stretch out before me.

And then the surgeon walked in. I held my breath.

"The mass is *not* connected to her brain," he said. Relief hit me like a wave. But then—*a pause.* "We'll have to wait for the biopsy results to know whether or not it's cancerous."

I exhaled, but I couldn't fully breathe just yet.

"She's doing well," he added. "You'll get to hold her soon."

And just like that, peace settled over me. It didn't make sense. I wasn't going to question it. God had answered one prayer—the tumor wasn't attached to her brain. But the tension still remained. The *friction* of faith and fear.

When I finally got to hold Zadie Ann, I prayed the same prayer over and over again. *God, I trust you. I trust you. I trust you.*

It took two more days before we got the final answer: not cancer. A rare internal hemangioma. Treatable. And, as only God could orchestrate, Vanderbilt had *one of the only* pediatric hematology teams in the country that specialized in this exact condition.

God had gone before us. He had worked out the

details long before we even knew we needed them. But that didn't mean the friction wasn't real.

This time the friction *stretched* my faith. It pushed me past my limits, past my comfort, past anything I had ever experienced before. I had never prayed harder. I had never *needed* a miracle more. I had never believed so expectantly that God would show up.

And he did.

It would be easy to say that the miracle was in the *good news*—that the answered prayer was the moment the doctor told me it wasn't cancer. But I have to believe that God would have still *been there* even if the news had been different. Because the God I know—the God I have *seen*—isn't just the God of perfect outcomes.

He's the God who meets us *in* the friction. Not to erase it. Not to fast-forward through it. But to sit with us in it. To guide us. To carry us. To walk us through the fire—not just to the other side but through every single step of the journey.

I know people like to say that fear and faith can't coexist, that one cancels out the other, that true faith leaves no room for fear. But I'd argue the opposite. Sometimes faith *needs* fear to exist.

Fear makes us desperate for our faith. It pushes us to the edge of what we can control, forcing us to reach for something greater than ourselves. It plunges us into belief, makes us cling more tightly to what we *know*—even when what we *feel* is shaky. Fear isn't a sign of weak faith; it's proof of our humanity. It's the flashing neon sign that reminds us we were never meant to do this alone.

Because faith? Faith is what we hold on to when the answers don't come easily. It's belief and hope in the middle of darkness, trust in the unknown.

Faith is the friction point of our soul—the tension between what is seen and what is unseen, between the weight of this world and the pull of something greater. It's that sacred, unshakable connection to our Creator, holding us steady in the very real, very messy reality of a broken world.

It's my deepest hope and prayer that as you read this book, you begin to see how God doesn't just *allow* the friction points of our lives—he *uses* them.

To refine us.

To redirect us.

To reestablish us for something even better.

Because the fire doesn't just burn. It *transforms*.

Two

THE *D* WORD

FAITH—IT'S MORE THAN JUST A PART OF MY life; it's woven into the very fabric of who I am, as inseparable as my last name. It's the rhythm of my childhood, the echo of Sunday sermons, the laughter in Sunday school, and the comfort of familiar hymns. But like anything deeply embedded in one's identity, it's *complicated*. My faith has shaped me, stretched me, and at times nearly broken me.

From the very beginning, church wasn't just a place we went—it was the center of everything. In my small hometown of three thousand people, the church with the tallest bell tower stood proudly on the corner, and it felt like home. It was where I learned, where I celebrated, where I grew. Sundays meant Bible study and big dinners,

Wednesday nights were for family meals and devotionals, and summers weren't complete without Vacation Bible School and youth camps that always seemed to involve some kind of skit about peer pressure and bad decisions.

I knew the words to every hymn. I could recite Bible verses before I could ride a bike. I could sing along to Kirk Franklin *and* Casting Crowns without missing a beat. I had the routines down, the traditions memorized. But even in the middle of all that certainty, there were moments when I found myself desperate for something *deeper.*

See, when faith is given to you from the very beginning, it can become more of a *script* than a *relationship*. You learn the words, you follow the motions, you do the right things. But what happens when the script stops making sense? What happens when life gets messy, when the easy answers don't fit anymore?

For me, that's when the friction started—the kind that creates sparks, forces questions, and demands something real.

Maybe you know that feeling too.

Maybe you grew up in a similar world, where faith was something you knew by heart but lived out by habit. Maybe you've found yourself in seasons of doubt, struggling to hold on to something that once felt so secure. Maybe you've wrestled with the tension between what you were *taught* and what you're *experiencing.*

If so, you're not alone.

Faith isn't always smooth. It's not always neat and tidy. There were moments in my journey when I wanted to walk away—moments when I questioned if any of it was real, when I wanted to throw religion aside and let go of the very thing I had always believed to be true.

But here's the thing. Something about Jesus held on to me even when I was ready to let go. His presence, his love, his actual message beyond all the noise of church culture—it was stronger than my doubt.

If you've ever felt like your faith was unraveling, if you've ever wrestled with doubt, if you're looking for something deeper than what you were handed as a child—*you're in the right place*. Let's dive in. Let's ask the hard questions. Let's chase after a faith that is bold, unshakable, and real.

WHAT ARE DOUBTS?

I have a few memories from childhood in which the word *doubt* rings a bell, but one in particular gave it the negative connotation that I still feel today. It was a Tuesday afternoon, and there I was, earning a badge for being somebody's plus-one to Jesus. My friend had invited me to her church's Awana program, which, if you've never been, is kind of like if Vacation Bible School and Girl Scouts had a churchy little baby. We played games, sang songs, memorized Bible verses, and racked up badges like well-behaved, Scripture-quoting Girl Scouts. We had a ball—and snacks! That day I was the living, breathing proof that she had "brought a friend," which—lucky for her—meant one more badge on that vest of hers.

My weekly church programming at our church was on Wednesdays, but every once in a while I got to church hop with other friends and today was one of those days.

After singing a few songs, we went to our Bible class in a familiar Sunday school room where Bible characters made of felt lined the walls. There was a boy in the first row with his hand already up. I couldn't tell whether he had to go to the bathroom or had something he really wanted to ask, but before I could find my own seat, he blurted out, "What are doubts?"

Which was a shock to me. I had never heard anyone ask a question about doubt because there was this common understanding, so I thought, that we just didn't talk about doubt.

The teacher calmly and kindly responded, "Doubt is the absence of faith. If you have doubts, you need to pray to have more faith." The boy looked puzzled, maybe because he, too, was feeling like that didn't seem quite right. At the very least, it felt like his question wasn't really answered. Instead, it was like we had been handed an equation: Doubt = Zero Faith

It was that simple. Faith and doubt couldn't coexist.

The subject was changed, and we held up our Bibles to get stars in hopes of earning our next badge, and we turned to that day's lesson without any more mention of the *D* word.

But I kept thinking about that interaction for days. I had always asked questions like that boy in class, but I had never gotten shot down in that way. It gave me secondhand embarrassment, and I took note about what was "okay to talk about" versus what I should probably keep to myself. I shoved doubt to the corner of my mind like it was a four-letter word I wasn't allowed to say.

Growing up the way I did, it was made pretty clear early on that there wasn't a lot of room for doubt in the church. It was treated like many things in the South: If you don't talk about it, then it doesn't exist. It was a taboo subject, almost as if talking about it could somehow make it true, like a bad case of the hiccups—ignore them long enough and maybe they'll just go away. Or like a scary monster—if you mention its name too many times, suddenly it will appear.

Faith was supposed to be an all-or-nothing deal—like sweet tea, which is, of course, acceptable only if it's actually sweet, and I am talking Bojangles sweet. If you had doubts, well, bless your heart, maybe you just didn't have faith at all.

FAITH AND DOUBT GO TOGETHER LIKE BREAKFAST AND BISCUITS

But the thing is, faith and doubt aren't enemies—they're dance partners, always stepping on each other's toes. I think having doubts and questions is as normal as biscuits at Sunday brunch—and honestly, they're just as necessary. The truth is, even the people closest to Jesus had their fair share of doubts. And if you don't believe me, just ask Thomas, one of Jesus' own twelve disciples.

As a disciple, Thomas was in Jesus' inner circle. He wasn't some random follower who had been picked up along the way. He was chosen by Jesus to be one of his twelve, which meant he spent three years as an integral part of Jesus' ministry. I can only imagine the number of intimate moments Thomas must have had with Jesus in that time, and the faith he must have had to give up everything he knew to follow him. But we don't get those details; instead, Thomas's legacy is marked by needing proof.

In chapter 20 of John, we find Thomas and the disciples. Jesus had been killed and buried in a tomb. Mary Magdalene went to the tomb, but the stone had been rolled away, and Jesus was not there. I can only imagine the shock, fear, and concern that she felt in that moment. She ran to tell the disciples that Jesus' body had been taken.

Two of those disciples, Peter and John, ran back to the tomb. John arrived first and stopped at the entrance, but Peter ran right past him into the tomb. Mary had been telling the truth: Jesus was not there, just the clothes he had been wrapped in for burial.

While Peter and John went back to where they were staying, Mary stayed by the tomb, and two angels appeared where Jesus' body should have been.

"They asked her, 'Woman, why are you crying?' 'They have taken my Lord away,' she said, 'and I don't know where they have put him'" (John 20:13).

She turned toward the opening of the tomb to see a man standing there. Because of the light shining through, she couldn't tell who it was. She figured it was probably a gardener coming to look after the grounds.

But it was Jesus, and as soon as he said her name, she knew it was him. Mary ran to embrace Jesus and he said, "Do not hold on to me, for I have not yet ascended to the Father. Go instead to my brothers and tell them, 'I am ascending to my Father and your Father, to my God and your God'" (John 20:17). Mary did just that. She ran to the disciples and told them everything.

Later that evening, the disciples were gathered. They had locked all the doors. I imagine they felt so many things on top of grief. Would the Roman authorities come after them next? Where did they go from there? For three years their lives had revolved around Jesus and then he was gone. Jesus told them he would come back, but what if he didn't?

Everyone felt tense and emotional, so imagine their shock when Jesus appeared and said, "Peace be with you!" (v. 19). Jesus held out his hands to show the wounds from his crucifixion. The disciples were overjoyed.

"Again Jesus said, 'Peace be with you! As the Father has sent me, I am sending you.' And with that he breathed on them and said, 'Receive the Holy Spirit. If you forgive anyone's sins, their sins are forgiven; if you do not forgive them, they are not forgiven'" (vv. 21–23).

But Thomas wasn't there when Jesus appeared. When he reunited with the disciples, they were eager to tell him that Jesus had come. "But he [Thomas] said to them, 'Unless I see the nail marks in his hands and put my finger where the nails were, and put my hand into his side, I will not believe'" (John 20:25).

It was at this moment that Thomas became known by the unfortunate nickname Doubting Thomas, like that one kid in Sunday school who just couldn't get with the program, who maybe just needed to pray a little harder. But let's be real: If your best friends came running up to you claiming they'd just seen a man you watched die come back to life, wouldn't you have a few follow-up questions? Thomas had just tragically and traumatically lost his teacher and friend. He was possibly fearful of his own persecution and trying to process all that had happened in such a short amount of time.

Just a week earlier they were waving palms and watching Jesus ride a donkey into Jerusalem. The emotional whiplash he must have felt! We don't know why Thomas wasn't there with the other disciples when Jesus appeared. Maybe he had gone to be by himself; he needed time to grieve alone. Maybe he had gone to get food or run an errand. We don't know, but one thing is for sure. We all respond, react, and grieve differently, so I don't fault him for that. I, too, like to go hide and be alone, but I also understand the need to keep up with everyday activities like going to the market or for a walk.

Thomas wasn't being difficult; he was being honest. He needed to see for himself. And you know what? Jesus didn't scold him, didn't kick him out of the group, didn't even roll his eyes, though I imagine everyone else did. Instead, Jesus met Thomas right where he was, doubts and all, and gave him exactly what he needed: proof, presence, and a little extra grace.

Here's my question: What if Thomas was wired to

need proof and ask questions? Because honestly, I get it. Some folks take things at face value, and others need to poke it with a stick before they believe it's real. Thomas just happened to be one of the second kind of people. And let's be fair—when you've got twelve different disciples, you've got twelve different ways of seeing the world.

A week passed and the disciples were together again. This time Thomas was with the group, but the doors were still locked. However, like the first time, Jesus appeared and said,

> "Peace be with you!" Then he said to Thomas, "Put your finger here; see my hands. Reach out your hand and put it into my side. Stop doubting and believe." Thomas said to him, "My Lord and my God!" Then Jesus told him, "Because you have seen me, you have believed; blessed are those who have not seen and yet have believed." (John 20:26–29)

I like to believe that at this moment, Jesus knew that Thomas would be an illustration. It's possible that Jesus knew Thomas well enough to know that he would need proof, and the whole scene was Jesus' way of doubling down on "I am who I say I am." He was good on his word, and he needed *all* the disciples to it.

When Jesus said "stop doubting," the original Greek

word used is *apistos*. Translated to English, we would use the words *unbelieving*, *doubting*, or *faithless*, but *apistos* specifically means not persuaded or convinced by God. As if there wasn't enough evidence to fully believe in Christ.

Jesus wasn't just speaking to Thomas's doubt, he was acknowledging that Thomas needed proof because he was not fully convinced based on the word of his fellow disciples. Jesus didn't have to show back up. He could have just left Thomas to try to work it out for himself. But I would argue that by showing up and giving Thomas the proof that he wanted, Jesus was not only meeting Thomas where he was but also showing the rest of the disciples that doubt is a very real potential experience. Thomas had been on the same three-year journey as the others. He had seen Jesus perform miracles and share the good news, but he still needed more. Jesus didn't come back to shun or shame Thomas; instead, he ministered. He made space for the doubt and gave Thomas assurance.

The Gospels give example after example of Jesus meeting people right where they were, through the good, the bad, and the ugly. However, if we have doubts, questions, or frustrations nowadays when it comes to faith and the church, we are often met with platitudes like "Just believe" or "It's our job to trust and obey, not to ask questions," which really gets my blood boiling.

There were twelve disciples who walked with Jesus,

listened to the same sermons, saw the same miracles, but you better believe they didn't process things the same way. Peter was all heart and impulse, jumping out of boats before thinking things through. John was the poetic type, always talking about love and light. And then there was Thomas—practical, logical, maybe even a little skeptical. He wasn't about to take somebody else's word for it, not because he didn't want to believe, but because his brain was wired to ask, "Are you sure?"

And honestly, I think Jesus makes room for all kinds. He didn't just call dreamers and poets—he called fishermen, tax collectors, doubters, and deep thinkers too. So maybe Thomas wasn't lacking faith at all. Maybe he was just the kind of person who needed to see things for himself, and Jesus, in his kindness, didn't hold that against Thomas. Instead, he met Thomas exactly where he was, with the proof he needed, like a teacher who understands that not all students learn the same way.

So, maybe doubt isn't the opposite of faith. Maybe, for some of us, wrestling with doubt and asking questions is just part of how we get to a faith that actually feels real instead of some kind of inherited religion that is more dogmatic than practical. I believe faith is meant to be transformative, life changing, and deeply personal, but how can it be any of those things if we never take it deep enough to see what it is truly made of?

THE OTHER *D* WORD

If there's one thing church folks love, it's a good old-fashioned "bad word." You know, the kind that makes everyone shift uncomfortably in their pews and pretend they didn't hear it. As we just discussed, for a long-time *doubt* was the biggest troublemaker in the room, but these days, there's a new word raising eyebrows: *deconstruction.*

Depending on who you ask, you will get any number of different explanations of what deconstruction means for Christians. Say the word out loud in some circles and one would think you just cussed in front of Grandma. People start whispering, exchanging nervous glances, like if they acknowledge it, it might come for them next like some sort of spiritual contagion.

Somewhere along the way, deconstruction gained a reputation as a slippery slope toward not just becoming a nonbeliever but being against Christianity altogether. However, what if we look at it as an honest process of figuring out what's real faith and what's just hand-me-down religion? Those who are deconstructing are often viewed as going through a crisis of faith, but I have come to know deconstruction as the process of asking a few key questions:

- What was I taught?
- What do I believe?

- Why do I believe?
- What does my belief call me to do?

Asking these questions can help us systematically work through our belief system. As we ask these questions, it's natural for others to arise, but the intention isn't to dismantle our faith; it's to make our faith even stronger. But there has been a ton of pushback anytime deconstruction is brought up in Christian circles.

Nothing made this clearer to me than the day a friend posted on Instagram about a podcast episode she listened to that warned of a new phenomenon called deconstruction that was—and I quote—"from the devil." If you could have seen my face when I clicked that link. Whew. Eyebrows scrunched, nose flared, that deep sigh that says, *Lord, give me strength.* I had a feeling the episode was going to be polarizing, but I was hopeful that maybe there was a misunderstanding.

I pressed play, hopeful I had made a wrong assumption.

Not even five minutes in, I felt that familiar heat creeping up my neck—the kind that comes when something doesn't sit right in my spirit. The two women on the podcast were adamant: Deconstruction, in their eyes, was nothing more than a progressive movement watering down the gospel, a one-way train straight to unbelief.

They spoke with certainty, but the more they talked, the more I realized something was missing.

They hadn't even defined *what* deconstruction was. No nuance, no exploration—just fearmongering and broad-stroke warnings about the "dangers" of questioning too much. And I had to wonder: *Who is this actually helping?*

Because if deconstruction is so dangerous, shouldn't we at least be honest about what it really is? Shouldn't we talk about it instead of treating it like some bogeyman lurking in the shadows?

Frustrated but hopeful, I messaged my friend. After all, we had always been able to talk openly about faith, and I wasn't about to stop now. Here's what I wrote:

> Deconstruction of faith doesn't imply trying to prove Christianity wrong or water it down, it's seeking clarity and asking the question "Why do I believe what I believe?" But it's not mutually exclusive to people with more progressive ideologies.
>
> One hundred years ago "progressive Christianity" would have looked like allowing women to sit in the same congregation as men; fifty years ago it would have looked like allowing women to teach Sunday school. It's not a new ideal or work of the devil to mislead or misinterpret Scripture.

> I would have really loved to hear an intellectual conversation on the theological differences or the pattern of progressive theology and its effect on the church, but this made it sound like the devil's work or witchcraft.

Crickets.

She read my message but didn't respond until the next day. And when she finally did, it was clear: This wasn't going to be a conversation. Her response wasn't an invitation to discuss or wrestle through our differences; it was a firm line in the sand. She fully believed what the podcast hosts had said, and there wasn't any room for another perspective.

I sat there staring at my phone, frustration knotting up in my chest. But underneath that frustration was something heavier: heartbreak. Deep down, I knew we were walking two different paths. Not because I wanted to, but because that's what the culture around us was demanding. These days, everything has to be labeled, categorized, divided into neat little boxes. You have to pick a team, draw your battle lines, decide who's *in* and who's *out*. And as much as I hated to admit it, she had decided we weren't on the same team anymore.

But here's what gets me: The thing those podcasters were so afraid of, the "evil" they were warning against? I don't believe it was in people asking questions or reexamining their faith. No, the real danger wasn't deconstruction. It was what happened *because* of conversations like the one with my friend.

When you start demonizing fellow believers—when you make *questioning* the problem instead of looking at it as an opportunity for growth—you don't protect faith, you divide it. And that, my friend, is a real problem facing Christians today.

Truth is, most of us didn't choose our beliefs like we pick out a new car. We didn't weigh our options of different religions or faith practices; we inherited them. They were passed down from parents, pastors, Sunday school teachers, and well-meaning church ladies with a casserole in one hand and a Bible in the other. And don't get me wrong, some of those hand-me-downs are treasures, but some? Well, some don't fit quite right once you start asking real questions and digging deeper.

Deconstruction isn't about tearing faith down just for the fun of it. It's about taking a good, hard look at what we've been given and figuring out what's actually true, what's cultural fluff, and what's just plain wrong. And if that makes people uncomfortable, well, maybe it should. Learning without asking questions is indoctrination. I don't want to be indoctrinated, and I think that mindset can be a lazy and dangerous stance to take. I believe that leaning in to the doubts and taking time to ask hard questions is an incredible way to take personal responsibility for your faith.

When I think back to that little boy in Awana, hand raised, daring to ask about doubt, I wish I could go back and tell him what I've come to learn: Doubt isn't the villain in this story. Doubt is just the starting point for deeper understanding. And Jesus? He's not afraid of our questions. He's big enough for them, patient enough for them, and, if the story of Thomas tells us anything, he's willing to meet us in those doubts and questions.

Maybe instead of shying away from doubt—or, worse, demonizing those who wrestle with it—we should be making space for the kind of faith that welcomes questions. The kind of faith that recognizes that God isn't threatened by our curiosity but rather invites it. Because if we believe that God is truth, then what do we have to fear?

Maybe, just maybe, the people who dare to ask the hardest questions aren't the ones losing their faith.

Maybe they're the ones taking it seriously enough to make sure it's real.

part two

A BOLDER, BRIGHTER FAITH

GROWING UP IN MY DAD'S PHOTOGRAPHY studio, I had a front-row seat to some of life's most beautiful and heartwarming moments. Families would come in for generational portrait sessions, with grandparents absolutely tickled pink to have pictures taken with their grandbabies. It wasn't just about the pictures—it was about preserving the legacy of family, the love and pride that passed from one generation to the next. You could see the joy in their eyes as they held their little ones close, knowing they were capturing something more than a snapshot. They were freezing a moment in time that would be treasured for years to come.

A few years later in high school, I found myself sitting in my first psychology class. I was captivated by how the mind works and how humans behave, but there is one particular assignment that stood out, one that felt almost like it had been tailor-made for me.

We were diving into the concept of *flashbulb memories*, and I was instantly intrigued. The name alone grabbed my attention. I'd spent my fair share of time around flashbulbs in Dad's studio and had seen those little bursts of light that captured moments in time. A flashbulb isn't just a pop of light; it helps capture a memory through shedding light to help create a photograph.

A flashbulb memory is one of those vivid, crystal-clear moments that etches itself so deeply into your brain that no matter how hard you try, you can't erase it. You know the ones, the memories that play back in your head like you're watching a movie, where every detail is sharp and bright, just like a photograph. Our professor shared her own flashbulb memory: the moment she learned about the September 11 attacks. She remembered where she was standing, what she was wearing, and who was with her. It was as though a camera had clicked that very moment and that picture stayed with her, replaying over and over in her mind.

We all have our own flashbulb memories, those defining moments that shape us. Some are happy: the moment your spouse proposed, the day you moved into your first dorm, the joy of seeing a positive pregnancy test.

But others are laced with sadness or shock: learning of a loved one's passing, the jolt of a car accident, or those life-altering, traumatic experiences.

These memories, they don't fade. They stick with you, whether you want them to or not. And as I reflected on my own life, I realized that many of my flashbulb memories had shaped my faith—those moments that left their mark and altered my path in ways I could never have predicted. Each one was a snapshot in time, a little moment captured forever.

Throughout this next section of the book I am going to walk you through many of the moments that are frozen in time in my memory and share how they influenced my faith. I warn you, these aren't the lighthearted testimonials you hear to make you feel good. They are the moments in my faith when I felt soul friction, and they each left me transformed in different ways. I hope they make you think and reflect more deeply on similar moments and experiences in your own life.

Three

SIX GLASS BALLS AND EVEN MORE QUESTIONS

I WAS AN UNUSUALLY CURIOUS AND IMAGINATIVE child—quirky, if you will. My mind was a whirlwind of ideas and dreams, often accompanied by my three imaginary friends—a story for another time—who tagged along wherever I went. As an elementary schooler, I was way more interested in talking business and politics with my grandfather than playing games with the other kids. If given the choice, I'd rather have a seat at the adult table during Thanksgiving or family get-togethers, much to the dismay of my cousins. My interests were a little . . . unusual for my age—like crocheting, watching presidential debates, and memorizing fun facts about far-off places. Did you ever watch Samantha Brown on the Travel Channel? I was completely *obsessed* with her.

Of course, I was still into the usual kid stuff—running around outside and catching *Power Rangers* on TV—but there was always a part of me that felt like an old soul with a dramatic flair. You know, a tiny human who seemed to operate on a different wavelength than everyone else.

Today, my eccentric interests, intense focus on certain things, and quirky habits would be classified as neurodivergence. But back then, I was just a chatty, curious kid who never quite got the hang of social cues. I would strike up conversations with anyone who stepped foot into my dad's photography studio, acting like a mini receptionist. I'd ask them what they were doing, where they were from, and offer up random tidbits about myself—just waiting for a real employee to swoop in and take over.

My mind, bless it, was always in overdrive. It wasn't the typical kind of hyperactivity where I bounced off the walls, though I *might* have done that a time or two. No, it was more like my brain was constantly running marathons, whirring away like an overworked engine. You couldn't see the gears turning, but I sure could feel them. And sometimes that mental energy would spill out at the most inconvenient times, and I'd be saying things when I shouldn't, asking questions at the *wrong* moment, and never letting a single second of silence hang in the air.

Nowhere was this more apparent than the day I decided to crash a church business meeting with my parents. While the other kids were probably playing tag on the playground or hanging out in the classrooms, I decided I wanted to be where the action was. So I plopped myself down next to my mom at the meeting, grabbed my own copy of the agenda and the budget printouts being passed around, and got comfortable.

The majority of the meeting revolved around finances—specifically, how to cover the costs of a new fellowship hall the church was adding. Apparently, we didn't have quite enough money to finish the job, so they were discussing possible fundraising ideas. This wasn't breaking news to me. I'd overheard bits and pieces of these grown-up conversations at home. But still, I hung on to every word like it was the most riveting thing I'd ever heard. After all, if all the adults were there, it *had* to be important, right?

As we sat there, each committee took turns going through their reports. I found myself staring at the spreadsheet in front of me, trying to make sense of the numbers and expenses our church had racked up. Honestly, it all felt like an alien language, especially considering I was just in third grade. But then something caught my ear. A voice broke through the numbers, and I heard someone say, "Ninety-dollar glass balls."

One of the ladies was giving her report on purchases for the properties committee. They were decorating the new addition's foyer, and according to the interior decorator's suggestions, they'd decided to buy—wait for it—ninety-dollar glass balls.

If I had been a cartoon character at that moment, I swear you would've seen my brain explode or my eyes pop out of my head. Ninety dollars?! To me, ninety dollars might as well have been two thousand dollars. That was an insane amount of money! And for *glass balls*? I just couldn't wrap my mind around it. These weren't even big, ornate things. She described them as about four inches in diameter, with no purpose other than sitting in a basket and never being touched.

We had just sat through a long discussion about needing to raise more money, and here we were talking about buying decorative glass balls for *ninety dollars each*. This seemed like a slap in the face to everyone in that room. Surely someone was going to speak up! I glanced around, looking for a sign that one of the adults was as shocked as I was, but the woman with the mic just carried on with her report. Then she casually mentioned there would be six of these pricey glass balls placed in a bowl.

Six glass balls at ninety dollars a pop? My brain went into overdrive. Ninety times six equals five hundred forty dollars. *What?* Five hundred forty dollars for glass balls that were just going to sit in a bowl in the hallway? No purpose other than to look pretty? My head was spinning. I could feel the heat rising up my neck, creeping into my ears. That was my warning sign—something was off, and I *had* to say something.

Now, I might have been a third grader, but I paid close attention in Sunday school. I knew all about giving to the poor, making sure people's needs were met, and being good stewards of our resources. To me, the point of church was to worship God and help others. So, spending $500+ on glass balls for decoration didn't sit right with me.

I shot a glance at my mom, and without saying a word, I slid my paper over to her. I pointed to my math, looking back and forth from the paper to her face, trying to be subtle—though I'm sure it wasn't. I gave her the *look* and then mimed raising my hand. She shook her head and mouthed, "No."

I knew what she was doing. She was trying to protect me from embarrassment, knowing that the adults had already discussed this and probably saw it as a done deal. But I had questions. I was a curious kid, and I needed answers.

Like a kettle about to boil over, my hand shot into the air. I had to ask. I glanced at my mom one last time. Her head was shaking ever so slightly now, but there was a small, resigned smile on her face, like she was saying, "Well, that's my Kendall."

The deacon chair—let's call him Mr. Smith—acknowledged me, and the room fell quiet. I took my chance and asked what I thought was a very simple question: "Why are we buying ninety-dollar glass balls when there are people across the street who can't afford food and we just talked about needing to fundraise?"

The room froze. You could practically feel the collective wince of the adults. Some looked like they might agree with me, while others seemed to wish I had stayed with the other kids. After all, I was just a child, and I was definitely sticking my nose where it didn't belong.

Mr. Smith responded quickly, trying to ease the tension. "That's a great question. But if you look at the budget, we already have money set aside for missions and giving to our community. Right now, we're talking about the properties committee and the costs for decorating the new addition of our church."

I already knew what he was saying—I'd been listening the whole time. But I couldn't let it go. I shot back: "I just don't understand why we're asking for money to help pay off the building when we're also wanting to spend over five hundred dollars on glass balls."

The lady who brought up the glass balls seemed a bit flustered at this point, and my mom reached over to give my hand a gentle squeeze, signaling that it was probably time to sit down. I'd made my point, but the question still hung in the air: *Why* were we spending this kind of money? And who thought ninety-dollar glass balls were a good idea?

Mr. Smith wrapped it up by saying, "Well, maybe we can look into getting some less expensive balls or other décor."

And just like that, the conversation moved on, but I was left wondering: Would they ever really reconsider what they spent their money on—or did ninety-dollar glass balls always have to be a part of the plan?

I wasn't thrilled with the answer I got, but I suppose it would have to do. As I left that meeting, I felt like I had done the right thing, though I couldn't help but wonder if anyone else would have ever dared to ask the same question about the purchase. I took the paper home, filled with all the expenses, budgets, and committee reports, and studied them like they were some sort of church homework I had been assigned. Bless my parents; they patiently answered every follow-up question I fired at them.

Going to that meeting wasn't about making a stand or stirring up any church drama. That wasn't my intention at all. But something in my gut told me those questions needed to be asked. As a child, you're taught that when things don't add up or you don't understand something, you ask questions to get a clearer picture. And, well, I was someone who always seemed to have more questions than answers and never quite figured out how to filter them. If something didn't sit right with me, I was going to ask about it.

Now, over twenty years later, I still think about that moment often. It's a memory that pops up when I'm talking to other young women who are interested in leadership or trying to find their place in the church. For me, that day marked the beginning of a much larger journey. My question didn't just end in that meeting—it sparked something in me. It was the start of learning how to speak up, challenge the status quo, and find my voice.

CHILDLIKE FAITH

I didn't realize it then, but the friction I was feeling that pushed me to raise my hand was the result of uncovering an inconsistency. How could we spend so much money on something that felt so unnecessary when there were people in our own community going hungry? On one hand, the church was teaching me the importance of giving, caring for the poor, and being good stewards of money. On the other hand, they were spending thousands of dollars to make sure things *looked really nice*.

That hot, tingling feeling of friction was manifesting as a question—a question that shed light on something everyone else seemed comfortable overlooking. I have to believe I wasn't the only one sitting in that room wondering the same thing. I was surrounded by well-educated adults who had consistently shown how much they cared about finances and the less fortunate, yet for some reason, they weren't raising their hands alongside mine.

Part of it could have been the desire to avoid rocking the boat, to respect the work others had done to get to that point. In situations like this, it's easy to assume that all other options have been explored and the choice being presented is the best one. But I also think it had to do with the fact that I was a child who didn't pick up on the social cues to just sit back and stay quiet. It never occurred to me that asking a question could offend someone or set off a chain reaction that might affect other conversations. I simply saw an inconsistency and wanted to make sure we were making the best decision for the church.

I wasn't thinking about what others might think of me, or whether it was the "appropriate" thing to do. I was just asking a question.

As Christians, we often talk about *childlike faith*, pointing to the passage in Matthew 19 where Jesus told his disciples to let the children come to him. It's a beautiful, poignant moment that illustrates how Jesus consistently went against the cultural norms of his time. The disciples thought that children would be disruptive to his teaching, a distraction to the crowd. After all, if the goal was to gather more followers, the adults—especially the "important" ones—should be the ones in closest proximity to Jesus, right? But in a surprising twist, Jesus flipped that expectation on its head. He welcomed the children, showing that in his kingdom the values of humility, innocence, and unreserved trust were the qualities to aspire to.

Verses 14 and 15 state, "Jesus said, 'Let the little children come to me, and do not hinder them, for the kingdom of heaven belongs to such as these.' When he had placed his hands on them, he went on from there."

Jesus tells us not to hinder or withhold the children because they already embody a faith that is pure, simple, and trusting. We often interpret this to mean that we should strive for childlike faith—believing and trusting in God with a sense of innocence and wonder. But I believe there's more to it. Jesus knew that by inviting the children to come to him, he wasn't just showing us an example of simple faith; he was also modeling how a raw, unfiltered, and Spirit-led response is not only approved by God but encouraged. The way children instinctively approach Jesus—without pretense or hesitation—reminds us that God delights in our honest, genuine responses to him, free from the layers we often build up as adults.

Without caveats or conditions, Jesus invited the children to come to him. He knew they would squirm, make noise, and ask questions. But I also believe he knew that their questions—endless and curious—were exactly what he wanted to encourage. It's simply who kids are; it's what they do.

Have you ever ridden in a car with a four-year-old? It's like a constant litany of questions: "Where are we going?" "How many minutes until we're there?" "Can I have a snack?" "Why are stoplights green?" You try to answer as many as you can, or you distract them with the right song to buy yourself a few moments of peace. But even in those moments, it's clear: Their questions are a natural part of their curiosity, an unfiltered desire to understand the world around them. Jesus knew this. He welcomed it, because those questions are a part of the faith journey—honest, raw, and curious.

It's simply in our nature to ask questions. It's how we learn about logic, reasoning, and the world around us. Our need to understand is often met with "Why?" and "How?"—questions that propel us forward in our thinking. But somewhere along the way, we lose that drive to ask, to challenge, and to push back. We start to accept things without questioning them, leaving behind that natural curiosity we had as children.

ASKING THE RIGHT QUESTIONS

I got a crash course in the power of asking questions during my college art history class. It was a small class—fewer than fifteen students—so there was no slinking into the back row and hoping to avoid participation. Each week we would dive into different art styles and periods, followed by lively or occasionally awkward discussions about specific pieces that our professor had chosen for that day's lecture. You never quite knew which pieces would make it into his PowerPoint, so I'd always cross my fingers that it was one I'd actually bothered to pay attention to.

One fateful morning, my professor pulled up *Las Meninas*, a baroque masterpiece by Diego Velázquez. Thankfully, I remembered this one. It was a royal family portrait featuring a group of children—a classic! I rattled off all the facts I had memorized, feeling pretty proud of myself. I mean, who wouldn't want to impress their professor with their *amazing* knowledge of seventeenth-century Spanish art? But my professor wasn't impressed.

"Great," he said, "but tell me more."

I stared at him, blinking. *Tell him more?* What more

was there to say? I had already told him everything I knew and pointed out all the "important" details. What else was there?

"You can't tell me more because you aren't asking the right questions and looking for the answers," he said, like it was the most obvious thing in the world.

Wait, what? I'm not asking the right questions? I had no idea I was supposed to be asking questions. I thought I was just supposed to know the information.

He went on to explain that, as art students and artists, we have to know how to critique art, and to do that we need to ask questions. *Why are the children standing in that specific formation? Why is the artist himself included in the painting? Who is the mysterious figure in the mirror? And if this was a portrait commissioned by the family, why is it an organic, almost candid scene, rather than a perfectly posed still image of the family?*

Suddenly, the whole idea of art—heck, the whole idea of looking at anything—shifted for me. I realized nothing is ever *just* as it seems. To understand something on a deeper level, you have to ask questions. The more I asked, the more depth and nuance I uncovered. From then on, my art critiques and classroom discussions became an exercise in challenging the surface-level details and diving into the heart of the subject. That shift in mindset was like flipping a switch in my brain. I started asking questions again, rather than just accepting things at face value.

And, honestly, I think our need for clarity is what sparks those big, often messy, sometimes uncomfortable questions we begin to ask about our faith and the beliefs we grew up with. We start poking at things, wondering if they make sense, wanting to dig deeper. The unfortunate part, though, is that unlike art, when it comes to matters of faith, asking questions doesn't always come with the same warm encouragement to keep going. More often than not, those questions are shut down, dismissed, or just brushed aside. And that, my friends, is a real shame.

RAW, UNFILTERED CURIOSITY

In a lot of ways, that third-grade moment with the glass balls was the start of something bigger—a little spark of curiosity that's stuck with me all these years. It wasn't just about asking about a church budget; it was about learning to trust my gut, speak up when something didn't feel right, and never be afraid to ask *why*—even if I was the youngest one in the room. Those questions, simple as they were, have been the keys to all sorts of doors I've opened since, whether it was in my faith, my leadership, or my approach to figuring out this thing we call life.

As kids, we're taught that asking questions is how we grow and figure out the world around us. But somewhere along the way, we start to hold back. We second-guess ourselves, worry about what others might think, or just get tired of rocking the boat. But here's the thing: Those questions that make us uncomfortable or even stir things up? They're usually the ones that lead us to something real and meaningful.

When Jesus said "Let the children come to me," he wasn't just talking about holding on to our childlike faith and wonder. He was saying that raw, unfiltered curiosity—those honest, sometimes messy questions—are exactly what we need to connect with him and the world. So, whether we're looking at a budget, studying art, or trying to make sense of our beliefs, let's remember: Sometimes the best thing we can do is ask a question, even if it's the one no one else is brave enough to ask. After all, it's those questions that have a way of leading us to bigger answers, deeper growth, and a whole lotta change.

The next time something doesn't sit right with you—whether it's a little weird gut feeling or a full-blown eyebrow-raising moment—ask yourself, *What's going on here? Why am I having a reaction like this? What conviction is getting stirred up in my spirit?* You don't just let it slide. You don't accept things at face value. You take a moment to scratch the surface and dive a little deeper.

It could be anything. Maybe you hear a piece of advice that feels a little too polished or convenient, or maybe you see something in your community, your work, or your church that makes you think *Hmm, that doesn't add up*. Stop and ask the questions. Why is it this way? Who benefits? Is there a different perspective we're missing?

I'm not saying you should go on a full-fledged, take-down-the-system quest—unless you're up for it, of course—but challenge yourself to embrace that childlike curiosity. Dig into the details, ask the hard questions, and don't just go along with the flow simply because "that's the way things have always been."

Here's the kicker: Don't just ask the questions *in your head*. You're allowed to speak up, to voice your doubts or curiosities. I promise, the world won't end if you ask "Why?" and *the people around you might just respect you more* for it. And maybe, just maybe, the questions you're afraid to ask are the ones that could lead you to something deeper. So go ahead, raise your hand, even if it feels a little awkward at first. You've got this!

Four

HELL ISN'T FOR PEOPLE LIKE HER

"GIVE ME TWO CLAPS AND A RIC FLAIR!" I can hear Zadie Ann shout from the other end of the house, her little voice full of excitement. Without missing a beat, Justin responds: *Clap-clap. "Wooo!"*

A chorus of giggles follows from Zadie Ann, and I can practically feel J's pride radiating all the way from two rooms away. They're not watching wrestling, nor are they reenacting WrestleMania. No, J, a true child of the nineties, taught Z that rowdy cheer when she was just a toddler. And now, a few times a day, it echoes through the house like clockwork. It never fails to bring a smile to my face, and I can't help but picture Zadie Ann, eyes wide and nose scrunched up, belting out that "*wooo!*" as if she's a seasoned pro. After their short celebration, they return to their LEGO building, and I get back to my writing.

It always strikes me how Zadie Ann, in all her excitement, has never actually watched *WWE SmackDown*. Heck, I'm not even sure she could pick Ric Flair out of a lineup, even though his name is practically a part of her daily vocabulary. But me? Oh, I lived in the middle of the WWE era when I was her age. It was *everywhere*. The commercials, the backpacks, the T-shirts, the VHS tapes, the magazine covers—it was like there was no escaping the men in their tiny hot pants, flexing and throwing each other around. It was more than just wrestling; it was a full-blown cultural phenomenon.

Now, Zadie Ann's "*wooo!*" is a funny little reminder of how much has changed since my childhood. She may not know the first thing about Ric Flair or the glitz of nineties wrestling, but in her world it's a fun cheer, passed down like some kind of quirky, time-traveling tradition. It's funny how certain things stick with us, whether we know the full history or not.

ALL WRESTLERS GO TO HELL

Unlike *all* the other parents—or so I felt—mine weren't into WWE or wrestling. And since there was only one TV in the house (ah, the good ol' days), Mom typically had control of the remote, which meant we were watching *ER* or *Law & Order.* Even when I tried to sneak the channel to see what *SmackDown* was all about, Mom would meet my decision with a swift "We don't need to watch that; they talk ugly." So I'd flip the channel back to whatever episode of *ER* was on that day, and before long, I'd find myself staring at Mr. George Clooney's charming face again, completely forgetting what I'd been trying to do in the first place.

But, y'all, my curiosity was *killing* me. My friends Casey and Trevor would come to school the day after one of the big events and talk about how Stone Cold Steve Austin was some kind of invincible superhero in the ring. They'd reenact the moments, throwing their arms around, pretending to give people the "Stone Cold Stunner" like it was second nature. And there I was, wide-eyed and clueless, wanting desperately to be in the know. I wanted to see what all the fuss was about. What did it mean to be "suplexed"? What in the world was the "people's elbow"?

With YouTube not yet a thing and no iPads in sight, if I wanted to catch up on the wrestling world and understand what my friends were talking about, I had to catch it *live* on TV. No pausing, no rewinding. Just raw, unpredictable TV moments that I could experience only if I somehow wrangled the remote away from Mom during one of those rare times she wasn't watching *ER* or *Law & Order.*

Then one day the stars aligned between my parents' work schedule and the TV programming schedule and I was staying with my grandparents. *This* was my chance. Finally, I could catch *WWE SmackDown*! My heart raced as I scarfed down my dinner, eyes darting to the wall-hanging clock every few seconds. Time was running out. I helped with my post-meal chore of drying dishes for my papa, then hastily excused myself, slipping into their bedroom where the other TV lived.

It wouldn't be long before Papa would be deep in a Braves game and Mama Dorothy would be in her chair crocheting. They'd both be occupied and wouldn't care what I was watching. I, on the other hand, had one mission: *WWE SmackDown*.

I jumped on the end of their four-poster bed and flipped through the channels, hoping to see the familiar logo pop up. Commercial, commercial, news channel, commercial . . . And then, *there it was*: the flashing lights, the roaring crowd, the loud announcer's voice introducing the night's event. Whoa, this was crazier than I had imagined.

If my grandparents had peeked in, they would've seen my mouth gaping open, eyes as wide as saucers.

I was *shook*. Straight off the bat. The theatrics, the over-the-top fandom, and those tiny shorts. Why did they wear such little clothes? Why were they all so angry? Why was everyone yelling? And what on earth was up with the Undertaker and his constant talk about *death*? I was legit confused. Oh, and the booing? Yeah, I didn't get that either. Why were they booing? And wait—who were they booing? I couldn't keep up.

I was only a few minutes in but already I could see why my mom wasn't a fan. I had no clue it was all acting. My seven-year-old sheltered self honestly thought these men had to be the *bad guys*. Yes, yes—go ahead and roll your eyes. I can hear you now. But for me, it just didn't make sense. How could they be good if they were yelling at each other and talking about death? I was convinced this was no way to behave; surely they must be hardened criminals recently out of jail.

I gripped the remote tightly, preparing to change the channel the moment I heard Papa coming down the hall to check on me. I wasn't really sure if he'd care about what I was watching—he probably wouldn't—but I knew for sure that if my mom didn't approve of *SpongeBob*, she definitely wouldn't approve of *this*.

I watched the rest of the match, absolutely amazed by their ability to throw each other around, wielding chairs like swords. I couldn't help but wonder if I could try a few of the "safer" moves on my four-year-old brother but quickly decided that would *definitely* get me into trouble.

As I sat there, I was introduced to new names like the

Undertaker, Triple H, and the Rock. Clearly I was witnessing a whole new world and culture that I had never imagined.

From my naive vantage point, raising your voice and calling someone names equaled *bad* or *sin*. I couldn't wrap my head around the fact that these men had chosen a profession that involved hurting others for a paycheck. For someone who loved good versus evil movies, life was pretty black and white in my eyes, and so far, WWE seemed to tick all the boxes for "evil" and "bad."

Still, there was a part of me that was thrilled to finally be able to report back to Trevor and Casey about what I had witnessed. Finally, I could contribute to the conversation and not be left out of the WWE talk at school. But, despite all that excitement, I don't remember ever trying to watch it again. Maybe it was the confusion, maybe it was the guilt of the whole thing, or maybe I just didn't need to see it again to feel like I was part of the conversation. Either way, that one viewing remained my only glimpse into that world.

Sometime later, I found myself sitting in Sunday school class, one of my very favorite places to be, led by one of my favorite people, Mrs. Lucinda. She was your classic sweet and graceful old church lady. Her gray hair was always perfectly set, thick glasses perched on her nose, and she was always dressed in ankle-length pleated dresses with tights—*even in the summer*, which I still couldn't quite wrap my head around. But bless her heart, she had this way about her that made you feel all warm and fuzzy, like Miss Honey from *Matilda*, except she was probably old enough to be Miss Honey's mama.

On this particular Sunday, we were having a conversation about heaven and hell. Now, I couldn't tell you what prompted it or which Bible story it came from, but I remember the question Mrs. Lucinda asked us: "Why do you think some people might go to hell?" I'm sure she expected a typical, thoughtful Sunday school response. But without skipping a beat, I blurted out, "I think just bad people go to hell, like criminals and WWE wrestlers."

There was a pause. She was stunned and probably holding back a chuckle, but I was confident. Mrs. Lucinda just stared at me, her glasses sliding down her nose a little, and I could see the wheels turning in her head, but all she could say was "Wrestlers?" She was probably trying not to burst out laughing, but she definitely needed more clarification, and I was more than happy to oblige.

I went on, explaining how I had recently watched wrestling, and in my young, eight-year-old mind, it made perfect sense that anyone who spent their time hurting people and being angry for a living must surely be a bad person. After all, being angry and causing pain for fun had to be a life of sin, right? And if they lived a life of sin, well, that meant they'd probably go to hell when they died.

I don't remember much of Mrs. Lucinda's reply, if she had one. It must've been lost to the depths of time. But what I do remember is how long I held on to that belief that wrestlers were "bad." It's kind of funny to think about now, but if you're a pro-wrestler reading this, just know I don't feel that way anymore. I still have a lot of questions, though, and maybe one day I'll get them answered.

If you think back to when you were seven or eight, you probably had some strange beliefs of your own. I mean, we all genuinely thought that a tiny fairy was sneaking into our homes to collect our teeth and leave a little bit of money behind. And let's be honest, most of us *knew* we were going to grow up and marry Justin Timberlake or Jonathan Taylor Thomas. Well, maybe that was just me, but you get my drift.

The things we believe and the logic we use to make everything make sense in our little minds form a crossroads of perspective and experience. For me, as a small-town girl, all the dots I connected just seemed to add up like a simple math problem with a clear solution:

SIN MATH: YOU + SIN = HELL

As a kid, for me the math of heaven and hell just made sense. Life was simple, predictable—peachy keen. I had never witnessed real crime or violence, and in my search for "evil" in the world, all I could come up with were felons and WWE wrestlers. In those early years of faith, everything felt certain. Right was right and wrong was wrong, it was clearly laid out, and making good choices seemed as straightforward as following a set of rules.

We had the Ten Commandments, after all—clear, unambiguous instructions on how to be a "good Christian." In my brain they were listed like a simple checklist with empty boxes next to each one. If I hadn't broken any of them by the end of the day, I could rest easy knowing I was in good standing with God. Looking back now, it's almost comical, but I can still remember mentally running down the list before bedtime prayers:

> "Well, I didn't kill anyone. I didn't steal. I didn't commit adultery—whatever that even means. I respected my parents. I didn't worship any golden statues. I didn't lie. I didn't work on a Sunday. I wasn't jealous of my friends' stuff . . . well, maybe a little. God, help me not be jealous of my friend's new clothes. Amen."

I carried this mindset well into my teenage years, treating sin as a simple checklist—things I either did or didn't do. Being a natural rule follower and people pleaser, I found more satisfaction in knowing I was "good" than I ever would have in breaking the rules. I leaned in to my "goody-two-shoes" reputation and surrounded myself with others who followed the same path.

Faith, in that context, was easy. When you grow up in a small town, in a middle-class family, with two loving parents, belief doesn't require much wrestling. A God who operated by a simple checklist made perfect sense. I had no reason to doubt. Faith was exactly what I had been told it would be: a source of comfort, a guidebook for life, a neat and tidy equation that always seemed to add up.

If you grew up in a youth group in the 2000s, you probably remember how it was shaped by purity culture, True Love Waits, and the ever-present warnings about the slippery slope of sin. We will get into the specifics of those programs later, but they were part of an overwhelming, constant conversation about sin and how it would ruin your life with one wrong move. Sin was framed as a zero-sum game: You either sinned or you didn't. And if you did sin and failed to ask for forgiveness? Well, hell was the inevitable consequence.

Nothing encapsulated this mindset better than a skit that took over YouTube in 2006, set to the song

"Everything" by Lifehouse. Nearly two decades later, it's still out there—pushing forty million views—but if you were around back then, there's a good chance you saw it when it first spread like wildfire across Myspace and youth groups everywhere.

The skit begins with a teenage girl walking hand in hand with Jesus, a visual representation of the beauty and simplicity of a relationship with him, enjoying the wonders of his creations. But as the song progresses, temptation creeps in. One by one, different sins pull her away—lust and sex; the lure of money, drinking, and partying; disordered eating; and, finally, depression depicted through self-harm and a suicide attempt. Just when all seems lost, Jesus steps back into the picture, standing between her and the darkness that had overtaken her, shielding her as she finds her way back to him.

It was powerful. It was emotional. It had us brainstorming how our own youth group could recreate it. I even believed, *If I could just show this video to everyone I know, they would turn to Jesus, and their struggles with sin would be over.* To me, at the time, Jesus still felt like the simple solution to the sin problem.

I wasn't perfect—I made my share of mistakes—but the struggles depicted in the skit still felt distant, almost hypothetical. I remember sitting at church camp listening to people share dramatic testimonies of leaving behind lives of partying and rebellion, and thinking, *Lord, will I ever have a testimony?* My faith felt . . . boring in comparison.

What I didn't realize then was that there were people very close to me who were struggling far more than I knew.

FAITH + SUICIDE

As I grew older, my understanding of hell—and who might end up there—evolved alongside my faith. My perspective on sin deepened, moving beyond the simplistic notion that it was just about choosing a life of short pants and yelling at other grown men. I began to see the complexity, the nuance, the gray areas that had once felt so starkly black and white. But nothing challenged or unraveled my beliefs about sin and hell quite like the summer after my high school graduation.

It was a typical Tuesday morning at my summer lifeguarding job at the community pool. The air was already thick with the scent of freshly applied sunscreen, mingling with the sound of the local Top 40 station humming from the radio by the concession stand. The water, still and glassy under the midmorning sun, reflected a calm that matched the slow rhythm of the day.

As usual, our one faithful swimmer—a preteen who never missed a day—had arrived right at opening time, jumping in and trying new tricks and yelling "Hey, watch this!" every few minutes to my coworker, who was currently his personal lifeguard. With just him in the pool, my fellow lifeguard and I took turns watching over him, trading off to keep ourselves from getting bored.

I leaned against the counter at the concession stand, chatting with the manager, absentmindedly twirling a loose thread on my lifeguard shorts as I told her about my plans to head to the mall later. I was on the hunt for the perfect swimsuit for an upcoming pageant, excited to find something that struck the right balance of classy and flattering.

Between texts with Justin, everything felt routine. Just the day before, he had gone back to school for his last week of summer classes, still riding the high from a weekend trip to the beach with his family. We had been talking about our next adventure—a trip to Florida to visit his stepsister, Ashley. He was in class. I was at the pool. Life was moving along as it had dozens of other days that summer.

The shrill sound of my whistle cut through the air, signaling break time. Our swimmer pulled himself out of the water, shaking droplets from his arms before grabbing his juice pouch from his bag. I reached for my phone, casually unlocking the screen to scroll through Facebook.

That's when I saw it.

A single status update from a classmate.

"Pray for Austin Johnson's family."

My stomach clenched.

Austin Johnson. That was Justin's stepbrother's name.

I stared at the words, my mind scrambling for explanations. It had to be someone else—Austin Johnson wasn't an uncommon name. But an uneasy feeling began to rise in my chest, creeping up my throat like a slow burn.

Without thinking, I refreshed my feed. Again. And again. Waiting. Searching. Hoping it was nothing.

Someone else commented, "What happened?" and the original poster replied, "His stepmom has passed away."

My heart sank.

Immediately a third person commented on her name, "Lisa."

It was Justin's mom.

The moment the words registered in my mind, my knees buckled beneath me. The strength in my body drained like water slipping through my fingers. Before I hit the wet cement, a pair of strong arms caught me—just in time. It was the manager's husband, ironically a long-time friend of Justin's family, who happened to be walking up to drop off lunch. His grip steadied me, but nothing could anchor the sudden overwhelming weight of reality pressing down on my chest.

All I could manage was a fractured whisper, my voice barely escaping my lips.

"It's her."

Mrs. Melinda, the pool manager, pieced together my broken words before I could even process them myself. Her face fell, her usual steady composure shattering in an instant.

"Oh, no."

Without hesitation, she grabbed her phone, her fingers shaking as she dialed. She was calling someone who could confirm the unthinkable, someone who could give us the truth. The pause between the ringing and the answer stretched into eternity, but when she finally got through, the answer came swiftly. Brutally.

It was true.

How could this be real?

We had plans. She was supposed to go with me to pick out a swimsuit after my shift. We were all supposed to be in Orlando in just a few days, laughing in the sun, making memories. Just last night we had been together. Talking. Laughing. Living.

And now she was gone.

My thoughts spiraled, spinning out of control. I couldn't cry. I couldn't move. It was as if my body and my emotions had gone completely numb, like a protective shield had slammed down, refusing to let me feel the weight of it all at once.

Then, a new terror gripped me.

Justin.

He was in Spanish class, sitting at his desk, completely unaware that his world was about to shatter.

What if he saw the post? What if he was scrolling Facebook right now, seeing the same cryptic message I saw? My stomach twisted at the thought.

"Was it an accident? It had to be a car accident." My voice trembled as I turned to Mrs. Melinda, desperately searching her face for an answer, for any piece of information that would make this make sense.

"Mrs. Melinda, what happened? Did they say?"

She just shook her head, still pressing her phone to her ear as she dialed my parents. I was eighteen—technically an adult—but in that moment, I was nothing more than a child drowning in shock.

I kept texting Justin, forcing normalcy into words, pretending that nothing had changed, because for him, it hadn't yet. He still had no idea. I held my breath, my fingers flying over the screen, keeping the conversation going, terrified that he would somehow stumble upon the truth before someone could tell him in person.

My parents arrived, their faces etched with concern, and the second I saw them, my facade crumbled. I melted into them, sobbing, breaking apart in their arms.

"Kendall, you have to hold it together for Justin," my mom whispered, her voice thick with emotion. "He needs you right now. Keep talking to him until they can get to him."

Justin was five hours away. Five impossibly long hours. But at that moment, it may as well have been light-years. The distance stretched unbearably, taunting me. We couldn't reach him fast enough. We couldn't stop social media. We couldn't pause time.

Frantically, we got in touch with his dad, who was trying to get to Justin's little sister. Justin's school had to be contacted. The chaplain had to be brought in. Someone had to be there when he heard the news.

His mother was gone. He had to come home.

The hours dragged, each minute stretching unbearably, etching themselves into my memory with painful precision. Even now, fifteen years later, I can still feel every second, the weight of them pressing down on me like a ghost that never truly leaves.

And then, finally, Justin called. His voice was raw, hollow, barely above a whisper. "She killed herself."

Three words. Three impossible words that made everything shatter all over again. None of it made sense. It never would.

Mrs. Lisa was the most faith-filled person I knew. She loved her family with fierce devotion, served in her church every week without fail, and radiated a warmth that made everyone around her feel seen and loved. She was the kind of person who sang worship songs while driving to the beach, who prayed over people without hesitation, who carried the presence of Jesus in a way that felt undeniable.

People like that don't decide to end their own lives. At least, that's what I had always believed.

The news wasn't just devastating—it was earth-shattering. Watching Justin lose his mom at just twenty years old was like witnessing someone's whole world collapse in real time. And the circumstances? They left us drowning in more questions than answers:

- What do you mean someone who knew Jesus could make this decision?
- What do you mean someone who prayed, worshiped, and believed with all her heart could still reach this point?
- What do you mean a prayer warrior, a strong believer, couldn't just pray the depression away?

People whispered. Speculated. Tried to make sense of the senseless. And in the back of my mind, I heard the echoes of conversations from my childhood—the ones that spoke about suicide as *the* unforgivable sin, the ultimate transgression, because how could you ask for forgiveness afterward?

But this wasn't hypothetical anymore. This wasn't a distant conversation about someone I didn't know, someone who had never known Jesus. This was *her*. Someone who *loved* Jesus. Someone who followed him, served him, and spent her life pointing others toward him.

It was 2011. I was eighteen. And people weren't having conversations about mental health and faith—not in churches, not in small groups, not in the spaces where they were needed most.

Suddenly everything I had been taught about suicide, depression, and faith wasn't just incomplete—it was completely unraveling.

WHEN EVERYTHING CHANGES

Have you ever walked through a moment that completely shattered everything you thought you knew about faith? A moment so profound, so disorienting, that you can look back and pinpoint it as the exact season when *everything* started to change?

Not just a small shift or a lingering doubt but a full-blown, earth-shaking, foundation-cracking realization that what you had once accepted as absolute truth was no longer holding up under the weight of your experience. The kind of moment that makes you question not just what you believe but *why* you believe it.

Maybe it was a loss that didn't make sense. A prayer that went unanswered. A betrayal that cut too deep. A suffering that didn't fit into the neat, packaged faith you were taught. Whatever it was, that moment—*that season*—became the turning point. The place where certainty unraveled and the questions started stacking up faster than the answers.

And once you step into that space, once you start asking the hard questions, there's no going back to who you were before.

In seasons like this, everything feels foreign and uncomfortable. It's like walking through your own life but not recognizing anything around you. The beliefs you've built your world on—the ones that felt so solid, so unshakable—have been hit by a wrecking ball, leaving nothing but rubble and unanswered questions.

In the middle of this particular season in my life, I came to a crossroads. I had a choice to make. I could let my doubts and questions pull me away from my faith, convince myself it was easier to walk away or shove my doubts down than to wrestle with the mess. Or I could lean in—dig deeper, ask the hard questions, and search for something more real, more honest.

I'll be honest—the easier option? That would have been to shove my doubts into the back of a closet, lock the door, and pretend they didn't exist. To keep going through the motions. To let my anger fester until it hardened into resentment. Because who *wants* to sit in the wreckage and start picking up the broken pieces?

But that's exactly what you have to do.

You pick up the pieces, even when they're sharp with grief, even when they're heavy with anger, even when every part of you wants to walk away from the mess entirely. Because somehow, in the sorting, in the questioning, in the rebuilding, you begin to make sense of what's left.

The best advice I received in that season was this: Nothing about life will ever be normal again. At least not normal in the way it was before. You don't go back. You build a new normal—one that holds the past but doesn't live in it.

That's hard when you don't like change. When you thrive on predictability and routine. But life doesn't ask for permission before it turns everything upside down. It doesn't consider your comfort before it wrecks what you thought was secure. And yet, in the aftermath, it leaves you with something invaluable: *perspective.*

Sometimes perspective shifts slowly—like when I eventually figured out that hell probably wasn't just reserved for wrestlers and criminals. Other times it comes suddenly—when everything changes overnight and you're forced to see the world through an entirely new lens.

It would be ridiculous if I still believed wrestlers were automatically bound for hell. It would be just as naive to hold on to the same rigid beliefs about suicide and the afterlife after walking through that kind of loss firsthand. Some truths can be understood only *after* you've lived through them.

And once you've seen things differently, there's no going back.

My perspective on sin deepened, moving beyond the simplistic notion that it was just about avoiding bad choices, steering clear of certain behaviors, or making sure my moral record stayed clean. I started to recognize the complexity of human nature, the struggles people carried, and the gray areas that had once seemed so starkly black and white.

I began to wrestle with questions I had never dared to ask before: Was sin always a conscious choice, or could it be something more subtle, woven into the systems we lived in, the circumstances people were born into, or even the wounds they carried? Was hell really the automatic consequence of failing to check all the right boxes? And what did it mean for people who had never even been given the chance to "choose" faith in the way I had?

For a long time, I pushed those questions to the back of

my mind, content to believe that the answers would come in time. But nothing challenged—or unraveled—my beliefs about sin and hell quite like the summer after my high school graduation. That summer, everything I thought I knew about faith, certainty, and the neat little boxes I had placed them in was put to the test.

Have you ever had a moment like that? A time when something you once believed with absolute certainty was turned upside down? Maybe it was a childhood understanding of faith that suddenly didn't hold up under the weight of real life. Maybe it was an experience that forced you to question what you had always been told. Maybe it was the realization that things aren't always as simple as we once thought they were.

Whatever it was, how did you respond? Did you lean in, asking hard questions and searching for deeper truth? Or did you try to shove it aside, hoping to ignore the friction?

Because here's the thing: Faith isn't about never having those moments. It's about what we *do* with them when they come. Changing your perspective and allowing yourself to see and feel beyond your current scope feels uncomfortable at first, like going to Pilates for the first time. Nothing feels comfortable or natural, but slowly you will start to realize that your capacity is greater than before and your understanding has been stretched further than you ever thought possible.

Now, on the other side of that particular season of stretching and growth, I have no doubts that when I get to heaven with all my questions, I will see Mrs. Lisa and get to share with her the seeds of faith God planted in me in the wake of this season.

Five

SEXUALITY, SHAME, AND MY BODY

AS A YOUNG TEEN, I ATTENDED A CHURCH class called True Love Waits. If you grew up in the early 2000s anywhere near a youth group, you probably know exactly what I'm talking about. It wasn't just a class—it was a full-blown Christian culture phenomenon that spread like wildfire across denominations, youth camps, and Sunday school classrooms.

The premise? To teach teenagers the importance of staying sexually pure until marriage. It was structured as a multisession program, with lessons carefully designed to scare the ever-loving hormones right out of you. We covered temptation, sin, and how your purity was a gift—a sacred treasure you would one day present to your future spouse like a sentimental, unopened wedding present.

And at the end of the course? You made a pledge. Not just to yourself. Not just to your parents. But to God, your friends, your future husband, your future children, and presumably all of Christendom.

The official True Love Waits pledge read:

> Believing that true love waits, I make a commitment to God, myself, my family, my friends, my future mate, and my future children to a lifetime of purity including sexual abstinence from this day until the day I enter a biblical marriage relationship.

I took the pledge seriously. I signed the little card with conviction, like I was drafting a legally binding contract with heaven. I even had my mom buy me one of the "True Love Waits" bracelets from the local Christian bookstore—because if I was going to make a vow of chastity, I was at least going to accessorize appropriately.

At the time, I couldn't understand why my mom seemed a little hesitant to fully endorse the program. I was so excited to make this promise—to do the *right* thing, to be *good*, to follow what I was being taught. So, why wasn't she just as enthusiastic? Looking back, I think she saw the red flags before I ever could.

Now, don't get me wrong—the intentions behind the program, and others like it from the big purity culture movement of the late 1990s and early 2000s, were probably well-meaning. But good intentions don't always equal good execution. And unfortunately, the messaging that stuck with most of us—the part that burrowed into our minds and left scars—had far less to do with love and far more to do with shame.

A PIECE OF BUBBLE GUM

It was January, and I was squished into a church van, packed in with my best friends, all of us buzzing with excitement. We were headed to one of the biggest Christian music events of the year—the kind held in a massive arena, complete with flashing lights, fog machines, and an enthusiastic worship leader who never stopped jumping.

This was the event we looked forward to all year. It wasn't just a concert; it was an experience. Multiple bands I loved were playing, and a handful of big-name speakers were set to take the stage. Some of them I actually *wanted* to hear from; others I knew would be a cue to hit the concession stand.

Back then, before YouTube, this was the only chance to see our favorite Christian artists perform. Otherwise, you had to catch them on the radio, buy their CDs, or shell out ninety-nine cents on iTunes for your favorite song.

I had been to a handful of these events as a teen, but this particular one? It stuck with me. Not because of the music. Not because of the worship. But because of a very specific message—one that would haunt my brain for years to come.

At some point in the night, one of the artists took the mic and launched into a message about "staying pure"—a wildly popular topic at the time. But rather than the usual "True Love Waits" script, he took it one step further with an illustration that still makes me cringe twenty years later.

"Think about your purity—your virginity—as a piece of bubble gum," he began. "You have this perfect, untouched piece of gum, still in its wrapper. It's yours. And when you get married, you can give that gum to your spouse as a gift. Because, really, who doesn't love bubble gum?"

I nodded along. Okay, sure. That made sense.

But then he kept going. "But if you don't wait until you're married, then you're giving away that gum to chew, and not just to them but to every person you're with. And when they leave, they give it back to you. You only have one piece, so over time, it gets chewed up, spit out, and passed around. Think about what that gum would look like after multiple people had chewed it. Pretty gross, right?"

I could feel the room getting quieter as the analogy sank in. "Now imagine that one day you find the most perfect person to marry. They're beautiful, they love Jesus, they love you. And when they ask if you have your bubble gum, you have to tell them . . . you do. But it's been chewed before. It's no longer fresh in the wrapper."

His voice dropped lower, his tone serious. "Do you think they'll still want that gum? Would you want that gum? Or would you want to throw it away?"

He let the question hang in the air, a dramatic pause that practically demanded self-loathing reflection.

"So, the next time you have impure thoughts, or find yourself tempted, think about that piece of gum."

Even now, just *writing it out* makes me want to crawl out of my skin. But back then? It made perfect sense to me. At barely fourteen years old, in the midst of puberty, the concept of "purity" seemed as simple as the DARE program's "Just Say No" campaign. It was black and white. Right or wrong. Pure or used up.

And so I wore my True Love Waits bracelet proudly—a constant, jangling reminder that my bubble gum needed to stay pristine.

GOODY TWO-SHOES?

A year or so later, I was a freshman in high school, fully settled into my routine.

Every day at lunch, I ate in the yearbook room, my safe place, then spent the rest of the period wandering through the common area, clipboard in hand, collecting quotes for the school newspaper. It was my little rhythm, my own corner of high school predictability.

At the time, I had been dating my boyfriend (Justin) for a few weeks. He was two years older, but that hadn't been an issue. My parents approved. We met in a school play, after all, and he was even attending the 6:30 a.m. Bible study I was part of before school.

That day, after lunch, I grabbed my clipboard and headed downstairs to find some upperclassmen willing to give me a quote about prom. I spotted a table of juniors in the middle of the common area and made my way over.

Immediately, I felt it. The side-eye from the girl at the end of the table. The slow *once-over* from another girl sitting across from her. The subtle shift in posture—the way conversations *quieted* as I approached.

Then, from across the table, a guy grinned and called out, "Hey! You're Kendall, right? Justin's new girlfriend?"

I knew who he was. *Everyone did*. He was the definition of a high school jock—breaking records in football and track, constantly in the yearbook for his athletic achievements. What he wasn't known for? His grades in math or English.

The snickers around the table put me on edge, but I

forced myself to focus on my clipboard. I was just here to do my job.

Before I could speak, the girl to my right chimed in, her voice dripping with fake curiosity.

"What does that bracelet say?"

She knew *exactly* what it said. She had *sat next to me all last semester*—we'd had *multiple conversations* about it. But here we were, playing dumb for the crowd.

I swallowed and answered anyway. "It says 'True Love Waits,'" I said, trying to keep my voice steady.

More giggles.

I quickly tried to pivot. "Could one of you give me a quote about—"

I didn't even get the sentence out before the jock cut me off. He leaned forward, his voice loud enough for the whole table to hear, his smirk fully formed. "Oh my God, that's hilarious. Does Justin know you wear that?"

The table erupted like a pack of laughing hyenas. And I knew. I was the joke.

I clenched my clipboard, my face burning, but I understood what he meant. Because while Justin attended Bible study with me, while he was kind and respectful to me, his reputation wasn't as squeaky clean as mine.

He lifted his eyebrows, smirked, and delivered one last parting shot. "Yeah . . . we'll see how long that lasts."

The words landed like a slap. Right then and there,

in the middle of the common area, under the fluorescent lights, surrounded by people who had already decided who I was, something settled deep inside me—a tangled mix of embarrassment, doubt, and something that felt an awful lot like shame.

I wasn't entirely sure what he was referring to. My bracelet? My relationship? Both?

But one thing was certain: I wasn't ready to let go of either.

Justin knew about the bracelet. We had talked about it from the beginning, and not once had he made me feel weird about it. He never pressured me, never tried to push boundaries, never made it seem like some inconvenience he had to tolerate.

But that table of juniors? They had already decided the rules of the game. And in their eyes, the math didn't add up. A girl like me—the Bible study–attending, purity-bracelet-wearing, yearbook-room nerd—had no business dating him.

So, I did the only thing I could do. I turned and walked away.

I didn't have my quote, but I didn't care. I could feel the sting in my eyes, the familiar prickle of tears forming, and there was no way I was about to give them the satisfaction of seeing me cry. I booked it upstairs to the yearbook room, practically throwing myself behind my clunky computer like it was some kind of shield. My face burned. My stomach twisted.

I didn't care about being "cool." But I hated feeling less than. Hated the feeling of inadequacy creeping in.

That afternoon I told Justin what had happened. He was pissed. "That's ridiculous. I hate that they made you feel that way." And then, even though he had nothing to be sorry for, he apologized.

I thought about that stupid bubble gum analogy. The one they had fed us at the youth event. The one meant to "encourage" us to stay pure because not only would it be sinful but we also didn't want to experience the shame that comes with it.

And yet, somehow, I was the one feeling chewed up and thrown away. How did that make any sense? How was that fair? To be made fun of for making what you felt like was the "right" decision. I wish I could say that was the only day I felt shame for wanting to wait to have sex, but it wasn't. It became an alienating factor in a few friendships, but I kept holding on to my decision.

IT'S NOT ABOUT WHAT YOU WEAR

A part of the conditioning that came along with purity culture was a heavy emphasis on being careful about what you wore as a girl. You didn't want to tempt the boys with your skirt being too short or by wearing spaghetti straps. Girls were taught to cover up, because *heaven forbid* we tempt the poor, helpless boys into losing control.

I know that sounds dramatic, but I actually bought a book at a girls' conference that said—with a straight face—that a belly button ring was a *gateway to getting into your pants*. I wish I were kidding. But like the bubble gum analogy and BlackBerry phones, it was just a sign of the times.

Meanwhile, where was the modesty talk for the guys? Spoiler: It didn't exist, at least not in any spaces that I experienced. A lot of the messaging I received was that a girl's body was her responsibility—but apparently, *so was a boy's self-control*. If a guy stumbled, the first question was always "Well, what was she wearing?" So, by the time I got to college, I had already heard the stories. When a girl was assaulted, instead of people asking, "Are you okay?" they asked, "What did you have on?" It was somehow always about the outfit or whether or not she had been drinking. And as ridiculous as it was, it stuck with me.

I went to exactly one college party while at Campbell. It was just a few doors down from my apartment, and even though I was wearing a tunic and skinny jeans, I still felt uncomfortable, so I went home.

Just a few weeks later, something happened that made me realize modesty was never the issue at all. It was dinnertime when my roommate called.

"Hey, can you come pick me up from my boyfriend's house?" she asked. She had walked over earlier, but now it was dark and pouring rain.

I had just gotten home from the gym, my hair still soaking wet from the shower. But I grabbed my keys, threw on sweatpants and an oversized sweatshirt, and told her I'd be there in a minute. I wasn't looking to impress anyone. I had a boyfriend—Justin—five hours away at his school. I was bare-faced and dressed like a homeless wet rat.

When I got to the house, my roommate invited me in while she finished cleaning up.

"You want a plate of spaghetti?" she asked.

Listen, when you're a broke college student, you do not say no to free food. I stood at the bar counter shoveling in bites, watching her wash dishes, and not paying attention to much else.

Suddenly I felt the heat of someone behind me. Before I could turn around, I felt a hand slip under my sweatshirt—and move straight to my breast. I froze. Every muscle in my body locked up; my breath caught in my throat.

He pulled me back against him, his other hand grabbing a plate from the other side of the counter like nothing was happening—like we were just two people standing in a kitchen, except one of us was panicking and the other playing it cool.

He leaned in close, his breath hot against my ear. "Let's go to my room." He laughed, like it was a joke.

His hand slid down my stomach, to my waistband. I felt the blood drain from my face. I couldn't breathe. I couldn't move. And no one in that house—not even my roommate, standing just a few feet away—had any idea what was happening.

Then, as if by divine intervention, she turned around and casually asked, "Hey, you want sauce on your noodles?"

That split-second distraction saved me. He jerked his hand up from where it had been inching closer to my underwear and answered, "Yes!" But before he stepped back, he took one last grab of my breast. One last invisible violation, one last power move. Then he strolled to his room, plate in hand, locking eyes with me before disappearing.

And he winked.

Like it was nothing.

Like I was nothing.

"You ready to go?" my roommate asked.

I still hadn't moved. I snapped out of it, forced a nod, grabbed my keys, and walked straight out the door.

The second we got in the car, she glanced over at me. "You okay?"

I lied. "Yeah, I think I'm about to start my period or something. Just not feeling great."

She accepted my answer without question. And in just a few minutes, we were home. I told her I was going to bed, shut my bedroom door, and let the tears spill over.

What just happened?

How did that happen?

Why did he do that?

Why did he think that was okay?

And then, the worst question of all: *Was it my fault?*

I felt gross. Ashamed. Violated. And I couldn't tell anyone. Because let's be honest, who would believe me? He was a baseball player and for whatever reason baseball players were treated as if they were "chosen ones" on campus.

If I said anything, I knew exactly how it would go:

"Are you sure you didn't misinterpret it?"

"He's a good guy. He would never do something like that."

"Why didn't you say anything at the time?"

I couldn't do it. It wasn't fair, I wasn't "asking for it," I wasn't putting myself in a risky situation. And then there was Justin. Would he be mad at me? No. He would believe me. But how would he react? Would he drive down and knock the guy out? Would he get in trouble? Would it turn into a whole scandal on campus?

My brain spiraled in a thousand directions at once. I

did what I had always been taught to do. I stayed quiet. I cried in silence.

And from that night on, every time I saw the guy on campus, he would wink just like he did that night, and I would immediately feel sick as shame washed over me all over again. I never told, but shame stuck around like a personal reminder.

MY CHOICE?

As a self-proclaimed Republican, in college I had a visceral reaction to the phrase "my body, my choice."

To me, it was synonymous with abortion, and at the time, I was unequivocally and without exception against it. I didn't even think twice about what the phrase meant beyond that. It seemed simple and, in my mind, dangerous.

But years later? I've come to realize that my reaction to those words wasn't about abortion at all. Deep down, I already felt like my body wasn't my choice. For as long as I could remember, my body had been a responsibility:

- a responsibility to cover it up so boys and men didn't sin
- a responsibility to shrink it, shape it, fix it—because it was *too big, too round, too tempting*

- a responsibility to keep it "pure," because its worth was directly tied to what I *did* or *didn't do* with it and how worthy it was perceived to be

Yet somehow, while I was expected to be hypervigilant about how I *presented* my body, men still felt entitled to it. They could touch it, comment on it, joke about it, degrade it. It was never just mine. It belonged to purity culture, to the church, to the male gaze, to societal expectations. I had never been given full permission to just exist in it.

At twenty-two years old, I was rushed into emergency surgery to remove a large mass and one of my ovaries. When I woke up, still groggy from anesthesia, the doctor gently told me, "We were able to save one of your ovaries, but you may never be able to have children."

I nodded, too drugged up to fully process the weight of what he was saying.

But in the decade since? I've had plenty of time to process it.

Because since that day, my life has been a revolving door of doctors' offices, tests, ultrasounds, medications, and second opinions—all in an effort to increase my chances of carrying a baby, manage pain, or determine if I needed a hysterectomy.

Every scan.

Every surgery.

Every appointment.

Each one was a brutal reminder that my body couldn't do *the one thing* it was "supposed" to do—carry a child.

Growing up, I never imagined this would be my story. I had always assumed that if you prayed hard enough, believed deeply enough, and followed the plan, you would get married and have a baby. It was a promise. Or at least I thought it was.

I'll never forget the first time I went to pelvic floor physical therapy. It was about a year after my surgery, and my doctor hoped it would help with the pain and discomfort I was experiencing from scar tissue and endometriosis.

I knew we'd be doing exercises and stretches to help loosen up my lower back and abdomen. I figured there'd be some deep tissue work, maybe even some acupuncture or something.

But what I didn't expect? The "internal physical therapy" portion. Now, I'll spare you the gritty details because that's what Google is for, but let's just say that "internal" means exactly what you think it does.

The therapist explained that because of where my scar

tissue was, this was the best way to help break it apart. I nodded, trying to act like I was totally fine, like I wasn't internally screaming at the sheer absurdity of it all.

But the moment I was half undressed, lying on the table, staring at the ceiling . . . the moment it actually started . . . the tears came.

It wasn't pain. I've had stomach cramps that were worse. But this? This was an emotional floodgate bursting open. I lay there blinking at the ceiling tiles, silent tears sliding down my temples, and all I could think was: *How did I get here? Why do I have to go through all of this, while some people accidentally get pregnant just by looking at each other?*

I was angry.

Angry at God.

Angry at my body.

Angry at the unfairness of it all.

But more than anything? I was ashamed.

Ashamed that I couldn't fix it.

Ashamed that, again, I had no control over my own body.

Ashamed that I felt so stuck.

Because for all the faith, prayer, and belief in God's plan I had clung to growing up, it felt like nothing but a naive pipe dream.

THE UNHOLY TRINITY

Sexuality, my body, and shame—the unholy trinity that shaped too much of my existence. I did everything right. Wore the right clothes. Made the right choices. Saved myself for one person my entire life.

But none of it protected me and I still didn't feel righteous or pure. I was still alienated. Still assaulted. Still left with a body that felt broken.

And at every turn, the price to pay was loneliness, with shame as my only companion. Because when shame is used as a tactic for righteousness, it cuts deep. So deep it buries itself inside you, until it becomes a dark shadow you can't shake. But now? Now I'm a mother. And I look at my baby girl, at her curious eyes and unshaken confidence, and I know—I could never bear the thought of her feeling this way.

I would never want her to believe her body is a burden.

I would never want her to think she's damaged or dirty.

I would never want her to carry the weight of righteousness weaponized against her.

And honestly, I can't imagine God wanting me to feel that way either.

So I began to wonder: What was the purpose of purity if I still carried so much shame? Why was sex such a taboo subject surrounded by shame and guilt if God made it to be a good thing? And, if it was truly a good thing, why did no one want to talk about it in Christian community, except to tell you that if you did it outside of marriage then you were committing what seemed like the ultimate sin?

Marriage in the Bible wasn't always about love or promises the way we often picture it today. Back then, it was often a matter of strategy—tied up in resources, survival, and lineage. Women needed men for protection, provision, and a place in society. Take Ruth, for example. Her story isn't a romantic fairy tale—it's about survival. Boaz stepped in as her kinsman-redeemer, not out of passion, but out of a cultural duty to care for a relative's widow and keep the family line going.

Or look at Abraham and Sarah. When they couldn't conceive, Sarah offered her slave Hagar to Abraham so they could have a child through her. That was considered a legitimate solution at the time. We read those stories now with modern eyes and nod along like it's normal—but if that happened today, we'd be shocked. I mean, no one expects widows to marry their brothers-in-law anymore, and in my struggles with infertility, it's never once crossed my mind to offer up a friend to sleep with my husband.

If the definition and expectation of marriage has shifted, then what has stayed the same? I think the answer is a covenant. If marriages past and present have one thing in common, it is that marriage is about a covenant between two people. A promise, commitment, and duty to each other. It's not a checklist of rules or a list of conditions. It says, *I'm in this with you. No matter what.* In Scripture, covenants are how God chose to relate to his people. Not through fear or shame but through promises. Steady, soul-deep promises that said: *You are mine. I won't leave. Even when you mess up, I won't walk away.*

And unlike the purity culture we were raised with, God's covenants aren't based on human perfection—they are anchored in his faithfulness.

Growing up, this was something hard for me to wrap my head around: that God was more concerned about my faithfulness to him than about my perfectly following an interpretation of a rule. He didn't demand my perfection in exchange for his love, and his covenant wasn't contingent on my performance.

Just look at the way God made covenants all through Scripture—with Noah, with Abraham, with the whole messy bunch of Israel, and then, through Jesus, with all of us. Over and over, he didn't make promises because his people had it all together. He made them because he's the one who's faithful even when we're not.

As an Enneagram three and someone wired to "perform" in order to feel like I am enough, it was hard to rewire and unlearn the way I believed that my purity was tied to my worth in God's eyes, but that was a shame he never meant for me to carry. If anything, I think shame is what gets in the way of hearing God clearly.

What I've come to believe now is this: God doesn't love us because we're pure—he loves us because we're his. Not because of what we do with our bodies but because of who he created us to be. I believe when we truly understand how much he loves us and see the innate value and worth he has given us, then we are given the gift of confidence and self-worth, ultimately allowing us to make the right choices for our bodies.

I'm still learning to trade shame for self-worth. But I want to teach my daughter that her body is a gift, not a problem to be managed or hidden or apologized for. Not in having a tidy theology or a crystal-clear doctrine but in reclaiming what shame tried to steal—and choosing, every day, to live in the freedom of God's love instead.

Six

JESUS AND ADDERALL

I AM A PRETTY DECISIVE PERSON. MY husband might argue otherwise, since I can never decide on what I want for dinner. But nine times out of ten, I make decisions relatively quickly, yet those one in ten moments are usually ones that require lots of prayer and counsel, and include a dash of anxiety.

Have you ever been in one of those spots where you're just stuck—wrestling with a decision that doesn't come with a clear yes or no, a clear right or wrong? One of those moments that leaves you second-guessing yourself, wondering if you're messing it all up just because your heart is needing something different than what it used to? Asking if God's still in it, or if maybe you've taken a wrong turn somewhere?

Shew, I sure have.

I was diagnosed with ADHD in second grade, and while my brain sometimes felt like my secret superpower, sometimes it also felt like something I had to fix. I had considered medication at different points but never actually tried it.

I had always thought of medication as something people needed for survival—for things like depression, anxiety, or other medical conditions where the brain needs extra support to function. And yet, somehow, I had never considered that my ADHD might fall into the same category.

But that all changed because of a baby bottle.

I was standing in the kitchen fumbling with baby bottle parts like I had never seen one before in my life. Do you know how many pieces go into a Dr. Brown's baby bottle? Approximately forty-three. Okay, fine—six—but when you're sleep-deprived and running on fumes, it may as well be a NASA-grade assembly project. Each tiny piece had to be cleaned, sanitized, and reassembled between feedings like some never-ending puzzle designed by a mad scientist who had clearly never tried to do this while holding a screaming baby.

Normally, I could have done this in my sleep. In fact, I probably had at some point over the previous seven months. After all, Justin had been gone for the last six, which meant all those late-night feeding, washing, sanitizing, and reassembling sessions had been tackled by yours truly. But that day? That day, those tiny plastic pieces were about to be the thing that broke me.

We had just come back from our midmorning walk, Zadie Ann bouncing happily in her stroller as we made our rounds through the neighborhood. The plan was simple: Pop her in the Exersaucer, assemble the bottle, feed her, then head upstairs for nap time. We did this every day. This was the routine—the sacred rhythm of our little world. But for whatever reason, Zadie Ann had decided today was the day to come absolutely unglued.

She was screaming. Not a whimper. Not a fuss. A full-blown, apocalyptic meltdown.

"Give Mommy just a second, baby, and I'll have your bottle ready, and then we can go rock and rest," I cooed, trying to sound soothing while moving at the speed of light.

She wailed even louder.

"Zadie baby, I promise Mommy is working as fast as she can."

My heart started racing. I could feel the back of my neck getting hot, that slow-building panic creeping up my spine. My fingers fumbled, slipping as I tried to snap the bottle pieces together. I knew how to do this. I had done it a million times. But today? Today, my brain had officially left the chat.

The more Zadie screamed, the shakier my hands got. The bottle ring wouldn't screw on right. The nipple kept flipping the wrong way. I swear, whoever designed these things was personally out to get me. I tossed that nipple aside and grabbed another one, but let's be real—the parts weren't the problem. I was.

"*What is* wrong *with me? Why can't I do this?!*" I muttered under my breath, frustration bubbling over.

Tears pricked at my eyes. *It's just a bottle. A stupid plastic bottle. How hard can it be?* But at that moment, it felt impossible. Like my brain had short-circuited, like I had run out of RAM and needed a full system reboot.

Zadie's meltdown was now at full volume, her face beet red, tiny fists clenched, her whole little body shaking with rage. And I knew what came next. If she got too worked up, she'd throw up. And if she threw up, that meant a bath before nap. And if she needed a bath, then we'd be even further behind, and I had a work call scheduled during nap time that I'd have to reschedule, and—

I couldn't breathe. The bottle still wouldn't go together. Zadie was screaming. I was sweating. And my brain? Completely broken.

I asked Siri to call J. I didn't know what else to do. My hands were shaking, my breath was coming in short, ragged gasps, and the tears were already mixing with the snot from *my* full-blown meltdown. When he picked up, all he heard was me—an absolute wreck—and Zadie Ann, screaming like her tiny life depended on it.

"What's going on?! Is everything okay?!" J's voice was instantly alert, shifting into problem-solving mode.

I barely choked out the words between gulping breaths. "I . . . *can't* . . ."—deep breath—". . . make . . ."—another breath—"a bottle."

Six months of solo parenting while he was deployed and not once had I called him in distress. Not during the sleepless nights, not during the blowout diapers that defied physics, not during the days when everything felt like too much. I had powered through every time. But today? Today I hit a wall so hard I might as well have left a dent in it.

"What do you mean?" Justin asked, his voice still calm, still steady, like one of us had to have a working brain in this moment.

"I don't know what's wrong with me," I sobbed. "I just . . . can't do it. My brain won't let me put the parts together."

It was like I had been handed one of those *impossible* wooden brainteaser puzzles, the kind you get in a stocking at Christmas but never actually solve. Except I had to figure it out while my body was stuck in full-on fight-or-flight mode, like a bear was chasing me—only the bear was my own screaming baby.

I had *never* felt this way before.

Justin didn't hesitate. He went straight into damage control. "Go look at the lazy Susan. There's a basic bottle in there—just grab one of those and make the bottle one step at a time. It will *not* kill her to use something other than a glass Dr. Brown's bottle for one feeding."

He had been home for a whole week, which meant he knew the current state of our kitchen inventory thanks to being on dishwashing duty. He also knew *me*. Knew that when I spiraled, perfectionism was always at the root of it.

Before Zadie Ann was born, I had gone full research mode on baby bottles, like I was preparing a PowerPoint presentation for a boardroom of pediatricians. I had landed on Dr. Brown's because I didn't want her to get acid reflux. Then I switched to glass bottles because I didn't want her drinking microplastics after reading one too many alarming articles. And now, all of that—the research, the choices, the pressure of wanting to do it *right*—was swirling in my already-overloaded brain, making this moment feel even heavier.

Justin knew that.

"Okay," I whispered, trying to force myself into autopilot. One step at a time. Just listen. Just do. But Zadie Ann was so inconsolable, her little body vibrating with frustration, her cries cutting straight into my nervous system. My own body was overloaded, overstimulated, and completely fried.

I couldn't think.

I picked her up out of the Exersaucer, hoping—praying—that maybe if I could calm her down, I could *finally* finish making the bottle.

"Shh, shh, shh." I bounced, paced, breathed. *"Shh, shh, shh."* I walked back toward the counter, trying to convince myself I could do this.

Justin was still on the line, now officially my proxy brain. "All right," he said, keeping his voice level. "Now grab the formula. Two scoops, you got that?"

"Yes, I got it," I said, still bouncing, still pacing, still trying to keep my hands from shaking.

"Great. Now just use water from the sink; it'll be fine—it's filtered."

I hesitated. I *did not* like this order.

Normally, I used purified water in the Baby Brezza machine, because—again—I had done my research. But we were past the point of breaking out the machine and setting it up. I had to let it go. I had to just get through this moment.

I swallowed my anxiety, turned the faucet on, and measured four ounces of lukewarm water into the bottle.

Justin didn't let me stall. He knew me too well. "Now screw on the nipple—it's already on the ring, you don't have to do anything extra."

No unnecessary steps. No overthinking. No brain-teaser puzzles.

I reached for the ring, twisted it onto the bottle, and just like that—the bottle was finally done.

The second I handed it to Zadie Ann, she latched on immediately, her tiny fingers curling around it, her frantic cries instantly replaced by the rhythmic sound of sucking.

Silence. For the first time in what felt like forever, the house was quiet.

"Everything good? Did you get it together?" Justin asked, noticing the stillness on the other end of the line.

I let out a long, shaky breath, exhaustion crashing over me like a wave. "Yeah," I exhaled. "I got it."

"I'll be home in about thirty minutes for lunch," Justin said. "If she's not down by then, I'll take over and rock her to sleep."

For the first time that morning, I felt like I could breathe again. I was still crying. Still shaken. Still feeling like an absolute failure. Shame sat heavy in my chest, pressing down like a weight I couldn't shake. I hadn't felt this confused—like my brain had just up and quit working—since college.

The last time I felt this way, I was staring down a math exam. At that point in college, I was trying to graduate and barely surviving under the weight of my schedule—taking twenty-two credit hours, photographing weddings on weekends, planning a three-hundred-guest wedding, juggling new health diagnoses, and hopping on flights to

Seattle whenever I could to see J. My brain had been running at full capacity for months, fueled solely by caffeine and sheer willpower. It wasn't until years later, after a lot of therapy, that I was fully able to unpack why that had happened, why my brain had shut down mid–math exam like a computer overheating and crashing. Turns out, it had a whole lot less to do with math and a whole lot more to do with stress—and how my neurodivergent brain was processing it.

See, when your brain isn't neurotypical, it doesn't handle stress the same way as everyone else's. It processes everything—every sight, every sound, every tiny detail around you—differently. Normally, I'm cool as a cucumber in high-pressure situations. I thrive in chaos, stay levelheaded in a crisis, and can compartmentalize like a pro when I need to.

But when too many stressors start stacking up? When life turns into a never-ending sensory assault of deadlines, expectations, and external noise?

That's when things short-circuit. And that's exactly what happened in that classroom. Everything I was doing caught up to me. Like hitting a brick wall at ninety miles per hour.

But here's the thing about being twenty-two and stubborn: You don't slow down just because you should. Instead, you tell yourself: *I can do all things through*

Christ who strengthens me! Which, in my case, meant I was about to push through in the most irrational, over-the-top ways possible.

Like regularly pulling all-nighters to finish projects and cram for exams. Like agreeing to photograph a wedding on the literal day of my college graduation—and booking another one the very next day—because the profit from those jobs would help pay for my own wedding. Like buying a last-minute plane ticket and flying across the country to Seattle the day after that second wedding, just to finally breathe and collapse into J's arms.

Was it sustainable? No. Was it chaotic? Absolutely. But when you're twenty-two, running on adrenaline and pure ambition, "rest" feels like something Future You can worry about.

At the time, it felt like survival. And honestly? In some ways, it was.

THIS TIME IS DIFFERENT

This time, I wasn't twenty-two. I couldn't just throw myself into work, distract my brain with busyness, or impulsively book a plane ticket to escape.

This time I was twenty-seven, crying in the middle of the kitchen, holding my baby girl, realizing in real time that this bottle fiasco was the final straw—the one that had officially broken the camel's back.

The weight of everything—J's deployment, the whirlwind adoption process, an isolating worldwide pandemic that kept me from my family, and a medical emergency with my infant—it had all been stacking up, brick by brick, until suddenly there was no more room for me to carry it. My lack of executive function, my absolute inability to complete the most basic of tasks—it was proof that I had reached my tipping point.

Not long after Zadie Ann finished her bottle, Justin walked through the door like a knight in dad-bod armor, took one look at me, and wordlessly tagged in. Without hesitation, he scooped her up, rocked her, and got her down for her nap like it was nothing.

Meanwhile, I stood there, still wrung out and shaky, knowing I had twenty minutes before I had to pull myself together for a work call.

But before I even thought about my job, I knew what I needed to do. I grabbed my phone and called the doctor's office.

"How soon can I get in?" I asked, my voice urgent, like I was trying to book an appointment for a life-saving surgery rather than a mental health check-up. Miraculously, there was an opening the next day.

Before I could even hang up with the scheduler, I was

already yanking open a drawer, whipping out my manila folder, and slamming the print button on all the research I had been hoarding. Because this time I was going in prepared.

I was terrified. Not of the appointment itself but of what it might mean.

I had spent my whole life watching people take ADHD meds, and to be honest, it freaked me out. In college, I knew kids who popped Adderall like Tic Tacs—pulling all-nighters, finishing assignments at lightning speed, and then turning around and partying like they had just unlocked some kind of superhuman stamina.

And me? I was already not sleeping well. And I had *zero* interest in partying. I just wanted to be able to think normally. I wanted my hyperactive brain to slow the heck down.

But there was another part of me—a deeper, more stubborn part—that hesitated for a different reason. Because if I'm honest? I had always believed that God made me this way for a reason. And if I went on medication . . . would that change me? Would I still be me? Would it turn me into a zombie version of myself like the kids I remembered from elementary school, the ones who were practically sedated just so they'd sit still in class?

But then I thought about Zadie Ann crying, me melting down, my brain completely failing me in a moment when I needed it the most.

And I realized—I couldn't keep living like this.

I had to set my pride aside and at least consider medical intervention, because white-knuckling my way through life clearly wasn't working anymore. Looking back, the signs had been there all along. I was drowning in symptoms and didn't even see it.

- The piles of laundry I couldn't seem to get through. And if by some miracle I did? They stayed in baskets for weeks, waiting to be put away.
- The half-finished hobbies cluttering my space—my sewing machine, my paints, my beads—each project abandoned mid–creative spark.
- The work deadlines looming over me, but the minute I sat down to focus, my brain bounced between tasks like a pinball machine. Everything felt urgent, so nothing felt urgent.

Thank God none of these struggles had trickled down to affect Zadie Ann yet. But let's be real—it was only a matter of time. I had two choices: keep pretending this wasn't a problem, or do something about it. And that time? I chose to do something about it.

That same afternoon, I sat down and opened a file I had been quietly collecting for months: a folder full of research, journal articles, and notes on ADHD in women. I had spent hours combing through medical studies, diving into how ADHD manifests differently in women than in men. I had highlighted symptom lists and scribbled in margins, underlining how my own struggles aligned more closely with ADHD meltdowns than traditional anxiety attacks. I had been tracking everything—sleep patterns, coping mechanisms, menstrual cycles—all of which seemed to play a role in the storm that had been brewing inside me.

I had known for years that ADHD was a part of my life—I was diagnosed back in second grade. And for twenty-six years, I had found ways to cope and self-regulate. Not always well, but I got through.

But today? Today was different. Today I realized this wasn't just about me anymore. Because what happened if Justin wasn't there next time? What if I had another episode like this, but worse? What if I was alone with my baby, and she needed me, and I couldn't push through it?

Since becoming a mom, I had felt it—how much my ADHD was affecting me, how my old methods of survival weren't cutting it anymore. Life before motherhood meant I had 100 percent autonomy over my schedule. I could structure my time, adapt my environment, and work *with* my brain instead of fighting against it. But now? My days were dictated by a tiny human's needs, and ADHD doesn't care that your baby needs to be fed, changed, rocked, and soothed on a schedule.

I had been waiting for my next doctor's appointment to bring all my research to my new primary care provider—who, thankfully, I really liked. He actually listened, which is saying something. I had a gut feeling that he wouldn't dismiss me, that he'd take what I was saying seriously. But what I hadn't anticipated was hitting a wall like this before I even made it to that appointment. And what scared me the most? Justin was home now. The deployment was over. I thought that meant things would get better, not worse. But the truth was, this wasn't just stress anymore. This was something I had to face head-on.

And for the first time, I wasn't just doing it for me—I was doing it for her.

THE APPOINTMENT

The next morning, I had a friend come over to hang out with Zadie Ann while I headed to my appointment. As I grabbed my purse, I also scooped up my trusty folder of research and documentation, clutching it like a toddler with a favorite blankie. Security blanket? Maybe. Shield to hide behind? Also possible. Whatever metaphor it deserved, I was grateful to have something tangible in my hands—something that made me feel prepared.

Walking into the doctor's office, I felt that familiar twinge of anxiety—not the full-blown *panic attack, I'm-about-to-run-for-the-exit* kind, but the *I-don't-know-what-to-expect-so-I-kind-of-want-to-bail* kind. There was a brief moment when I considered turning around and rescheduling. Maybe pushing it out a few weeks? Maybe indefinitely? My nervous system has never been a fan of big changes, and when given the option, I will almost always opt out of discomfort.

But deep down, I knew I couldn't keep putting this off.

The nurse called my name, and I followed her to the scale of doom. I stepped on, peeked at the number, and immediately thought, *Yikes. That was not what I was prepared to see.*

I wasn't surprised, though. My weight has always run parallel to my stress levels, and given the past year? It made sense. J's deployment, the lightning-fast adoption process, the worldwide pandemic's resulting isolation, and a surprise medical emergency with my baby—it had all been taking up space. And apparently, my body had decided to store it for later.

We made our way to the exam room, where I climbed onto the exam table, still gripping my folder with a white-knuckled death grip. To anyone else, it was just a manila folder filled with documents, but to me? It was proof.

Proof that I wasn't making this up.

Proof that I had done my homework.

Proof that I deserved to be believed.

While I waited, I ran through the doctor's stats in my head like I was reviewing a player lineup before a game.

- Born in Illinois
- Completed residency at UCLA Northridge
- Been practicing since 1999
- Specializes in preventive medicine, which I liked
- Has logged over three hundred hours of volunteer service with a Christian medical ministry, which told me he believed in both science *and* faith

I had learned all of this before even making the appointment. One of the joys—or, let's be honest, *pains*—of moving so often is constantly having to find new doctors, dentists, mechanics, and hair stylists, so for me, it's basically turned into a research project / personal challenge to find the best one. Some people doomscroll social media. I deep-dive on professionals I might need to book an appointment with.

Knowing these little details about my doctor helped calm my nerves. Just like my folder, information has always been a comforting vice for me. You can bet money that when I walk onto a car lot, I already know more about the vehicle than the salesperson does. In high school, I had memorized every single NC State basketball starter—including their free throw percentages, playing time, points per game, even their height, weight, and major. While I waited for the doctor, I went over his stats the same way I once rattled off ACC player bios.

A soft knock at the door pulled me from my mental ramblings. The doctor walked in with a friendly smile and took a seat. I don't know whether the nurse had warned him about my folder or he just immediately sensed its power, but after a brief exchange of pleasantries, his eyes flicked down to it.

"So, what's in the folder?" he asked, amused.

He already knew why I was there—it was in my chart—so I didn't hesitate. I launched directly into my findings like I was presenting a thesis defense on ADHD and women's health.

I talked. A lot. He nodded, occasionally interjecting with a question, but mostly he just listened. I told him about my ADHD diagnosis from childhood. How I had managed to cope without medication for years. How past doctors had been quick to treat me for anxiety and panic attacks but had never dug deeper into the root of the issue.

I walked him through my research on ADHD in women—the medical journals, the documented symptoms that aligned more with my experiences than generalized anxiety ever had. I had even made notes on different medication options based on my symptoms, along with a journal tracking my sleep patterns and coping mechanisms, and how my cycle seemed to affect my symptoms.

I can only imagine what was running through his head as I info-dumped on him for a solid fifteen minutes.

By the time I finally reached the end of my informal TED Talk, I realized my shoulders had relaxed. The tension that had been sitting there for days was finally melting away.

I felt seen. And honestly? That felt like a win no matter what came next.

He leaned back in his chair, nodding thoughtfully, and said the words I had been holding my breath for. "I think you're right. And I think we should try medication—if you're ready."

I swallowed hard. "I think I'm ready," I admitted. "But I'm nervous. I don't want it to mess with my sleep, and I don't want it to speed up my brain even more."

He nodded. "If you really need the medication, that won't happen," he assured me. "In fact, it should actually help slow things down."

I took a deep breath and nodded back. He wrote the prescription, and immediately my anxiety about the appointment shifted to nervous anticipation for what came next. I agreed to come back in a week for a follow-up, but he also said he'd personally call me the next day to check in after my first two doses.

And just like that, everything was about to change.

I left the doctor's office feeling nervous but encouraged, my mind buzzing as I pulled into the Chick-fil-A drive-through for a much-needed late breakfast. Nothing says *processing life changes* like chicken minis and a large sweet tea.

As I waited for my order, I called Justin, replaying the entire appointment for him, word for word, like he was an audience member at my one-woman show.

"Babe, I don't feel crazy. I don't feel broken. I feel . . . validated." The emotion cracked through my voice.

Justin listened, letting me get it all out. Then I called my mom and did the exact same thing, because when something big happens, you have to debrief with the people who just *get* you.

By the time I had picked up my prescription from Publix and made it home, I felt a mix of cautious hope and absolute terror. I held the bottle in my hand, staring at it like it held the answers to the universe. Then, before I could overthink myself into oblivion, I took my first pill.

Now, we wait.

Zadie Ann and I went for a walk while I waited to see if anything would happen. It was a perfect, warm Friday afternoon, and Justin would be home soon since he got off early. As we strolled down the sidewalk, about fifteen minutes in, I felt it.

It was bizarre.

I could almost feel the cogs in my brain slowing down, like a machine finally getting the oil it had needed for years. The constant background noise—the never-ending loop of feedback, analysis, narration, and overthinking was . . . quieter. Not gone. But noticeably quieter.

By the time we made it back to the house, Justin was pulling into the driveway. He barely had the truck in park before he asked, "Can you tell a difference yet?"

I tried to put it into words. "Yeah . . . it's weird. Like, my brain isn't running a marathon at all times. Everything is . . . quieter?"

His face lit up. "That's great! I'm so glad!" he exclaimed.

Bless him. He really was genuinely happy for me. Even though he has never been able to fully relate to the way my brain works, he has always been patient, kind, and incredibly supportive. He can tell when I'm overwhelmed and dysregulated, and he's never once pushed me to try medication. But I think deep down, he was relieved. Because he hates to see me struggle.

"Actually," I told him, "I think I feel like I could go rest."

Which was wild—because I don't nap. Ever. Over the past three nights, I had barely gotten a collective eight hours of sleep, and yet I had been running on sheer willpower and caffeine.

Justin didn't hesitate. "I think that's a great idea. I've got the baby. Go."

And I did. I went upstairs, crawled into bed, and fully expected to just lie there staring at the ceiling, overanalyzing whether or not the medicine was "working." Instead? I was out like a light. And not just *asleep*, but the deep, motionless, drooling-like-a-dead-animal kind of sleep.

It felt like seconds passed before I felt Justin's hand gently patting my leg. "Hey, just wanted to check on you. You've been asleep for four hours, and I wanted to make sure you're okay."

I blinked, coming back from another planet. "Four hours?! No way."

But the clock didn't lie. It was real. The medication was working. And for the first time in a long time, I knew I was going to be okay.

THE FRICTION POINT

I often reflected on my hesitation to try medication. *What if I had gone on it sooner? What would it have changed?*

Was taking medication now hindering some of the gifts God had given me?

And maybe the biggest question of all: *What does God think about me taking medicine for something that isn't technically an illness?*

It's not like I had cancer or an infection. It wasn't life-threatening. But it *was* a medication that altered how my brain functioned, and that seemed different.

In church we're told to look to the Bible for answers, but this one wasn't so clear-cut. After all, there weren't ADHD meds in Jesus' time. There was no verse in Leviticus that said, "Thou shalt take thy stimulant and stop forgetting where thou put thy keys." I so badly wished there was. But I wasn't going to find one. And yet I don't think you have to personally wrestle with the ADHD medication question to understand what it's like to struggle with internal turmoil.

I think we've all had those seasons—the ones where we're standing at a crossroads, tension pressing in from both sides, trying to make a decision that doesn't have a clear answer laid out in Scripture. And to complicate things further, sometimes the church itself doesn't even have a unified stance on the issue at hand.

How do you make a decision that aligns with your faith when there's no black-and-white answer?

For me, it took time. A lot of conversations with my

therapist, a lot of prayer, and a whole lot of reframing how I viewed my ADHD. It took a while for me to break down the shame I carried around not being able to "fix" my ADHD with sheer willpower, spiritual practices, and a handful of organization hacks. Somewhere along the way, I had internalized the idea that *my righteousness as a believer was directly tied to my ability to stay organized.*

Let that sink in for a second.

At some point in my life, I had taken the old saying "cleanliness is next to godliness," run with it, and turned it into a moral failure every time my laundry piled up or my office looked like a crime scene.

And here's the kicker—that belief created a lose-lose cycle for me.

- When I was struggling, I felt shame for not being more disciplined, for not having my life in order.
- But when I *did* manage to keep everything together, I felt pride—and worse, I found myself looking down on others who couldn't manage as well.

It was toxic.

And the worst part? I had never questioned it before. I had indiscriminately absorbed this idea that my ability—or inability—to keep my life together had some direct link to my spiritual worth.

That had to change.

So, I studied Scripture. I worked through unlearning the lies that had been filling me with shame. I dug into what God *actually* says about our struggles, our limitations, and his grace. I did the work. And you know what I found? That nowhere in Scripture does God expect perfection from me. We are called to be good stewards of what we have, yes—but God isn't disappointed in me for struggling with executive functioning.

Have you ever been there? Maybe it wasn't ADHD medication for you. Maybe it was starting therapy after years of believing you just needed to "pray harder." Maybe it was setting a boundary that made you feel guilty but was the only way to protect your peace. Maybe it was walking away from a belief, a system, or even a relationship that no longer aligned with who you were becoming.

Whatever it was, I bet you felt it—that friction, that internal battle, that nagging voice asking, *But what if this means I'm not trusting God enough?* If you have, I want you to hear this: God can handle your big emotions, meltdowns, and wrestling. He is not sitting in heaven, arms crossed, disappointed that you need help, that you need support, that you need something outside of sheer willpower to function.

If you are at a crossroads, stuck in uncertainty, tangled in the fear of making the wrong choice, I encourage you to bring it to God honestly. Not the filtered, polished, Sunday-morning version but the real, raw, unfiltered version.

Ask yourself:

- Have I internalized beliefs that aren't actually from God but from cultural expectations?
- Is this decision leading me toward healing and wholeness or further into fear?

Because I don't believe God calls us to live in turmoil over decisions that are ultimately about taking care of the minds and bodies he gave us.

I pray that whatever you're wrestling with today, you won't hold on to guilt as tightly as I did. Because sometimes the thing we think will change us for the worse is actually the thing that sets us free.

Seven

WHAT HAPPENS WHEN CHRISTIANS DON'T LOOK LIKE CHRIST

REMEMBER HOW I USED TO THINK ALL WRESTLERS were bad and going to hell? Well, I also believed that all Christians were good and only did "good" things. The difference is that little myth didn't get busted back in elementary school. Unfortunately, that realization came much more recently.

"The good guys always win. Right, Mommy?" Zadie Ann's voice piped up from the back seat, full of preschool conviction.

We were on the way to school, and she had just given

me a full breakdown of the new *PAW Patrol* movie, complete with gasps, sound effects, and the kind of hand gestures that made me wish I had rearview-mirror wipers. In great detail, she explained how Mayor Humdinger—who, according to her, was *always* up to *no good*—had been out-badded this time.

"There's an even *bigger* bad guy, Mommy!" she announced, voice brimming with dramatic intensity. A *woman* villain, no less—a scientist who was trying to steal the PAW Patrol's superpowers.

I made all the right mom noises: *Oh wow! No way! She tried to steal their powers?!*

But when she got to the meteors—the ones that were about to destroy the whole city—her voice grew tight with excitement. "Remember, Mommy?! The part where I had to get in your lap at the movie theater?!"

Oh, I remembered. Because at that very moment, Skye—the tiniest, bravest pup—rose to the challenge, blasting and redirecting the meteors just in time. And just like that, the city was saved.

Tension resolved. Disaster averted. The good guys won. Which, of course, led to her question: "Right, Mommy? Like on PAW Patrol, the good guys always win!"

I hesitated. She took my silence as a need for emphasis.

"Right, Mommy?! The good guys *always* win?!"

I could hear the certainty in her voice. The *hope*. The

absolute belief in a world where good triumphs over evil—where heroes always save the day just in the nick of time. And I wanted so badly for that to be true.

"Yes, you're right, sweetie," I answered, forcing a smile.

But in the back of my mind, the answer I didn't say settled deep in my chest.

No, baby . . . not always.

THE ULTIMATE GOOD GUYS

Growing up, you just know the good guys always win. It's in the movies. It's in the bedtime stories. It's in the way your parents talk about right and wrong like there's a clear-cut scoreboard—like life is just one big superhero showdown and the bad guys always lose in the end.

And if there was ever an ultimate good team, it was Christians.

We were supposed to be the ones who showed up. The helpers, the givers, the ones who stepped in at just the right moment. We were supposed to love people without expecting anything in return.

And I truly believe that is who we are called to be, the good guys, but unfortunately, I discovered that we often miss the mark, and not just by a little.

So many things cracked wide open in 2020, including

me. In my own little world, everything felt like it had changed overnight. My life was completely unrecognizable from the year before, but even in the chaos, I was settling into my new role as a mom.

In the middle of lockdown, we finalized Zadie Ann's adoption over Zoom, and I felt the weight of seeing our prayers answered while also wanting to raise Zadie Ann well in honor of her bio mom's decision to choose us as her parents.

Before becoming a mom, I had done all the research. I knew the best swaddles, the safest car seats, the difference between paced bottle feeding and dream feeds. I had listened to every baby sleep expert on Instagram, learned the proper way to burp a newborn—spoiler: turns out, it's not one-size-fits-all—and could recite baby CPR in my sleep.

But adoption? That was a whole different level of preparation.

It's not just setting up a nursery and picking out the softest baby blankets; it's home studies, background checks, hours of training, and an interrogation-level deep dive into every aspect of your life. You have to prove you'll be a good parent—not just in the way every expectant parent wonders if they'll measure up, but on paper, to agencies, social workers, and lawyers. You gather financial records, medical histories, references from friends, fingerprint scans. You even get asked about your childhood, your marriage, how you plan to discipline, and how you'll incorporate the child's biological family into their life.

It's deeply personal and wildly invasive, but at the heart of it all is a child who deserves the very best home possible. And beyond the paperwork, there's the emotional preparation—learning about attachment, trauma, loss, and how even the best adoption story starts with heartbreak. It's waiting, hoping, preparing, and holding your breath—because unlike pregnancy, where you have a due date, adoption comes with no guarantees and no timeline. It's stepping out in faith, with your arms and heart wide open, hoping that one day soon you'll finally get to say, "Welcome home, baby."

Before we started the adoption process, I used to think "color blindness" was a *good* thing. I thought if we just loved each other, if we didn't "see" race, that would somehow be enough. I thought not acknowledging skin color was the way to ensure fairness, unity, and equality. But the deeper I got into this journey, the more I realized how dismissive and harmful that mindset actually is. Because saying "I don't see color" is really just another way of saying "I don't see the beauty in the different shades God created."

It ignores the richness of culture.

It ignores the weight of history.

It ignores the very real, lived experiences that come with race.

And for my child? Ignoring any part of who she is wasn't an option. She deserved to be seen in full color.

We took classes on natural hair care, and I sought out Black doctors and providers to try to be as prepared as possible for her arrival, but there was one thing I couldn't have prepared myself for, and that was good old-fashioned racism.

I quickly realized racism wasn't just "a thing of the past." And let me tell you—I didn't need a book or a seminar to teach me that. I experienced it firsthand.

I experienced it in the way people's eyes lingered a little too long when I walked into a store with my baby on my hip. In the way strangers asked intrusive, inappropriate questions about where she was from. In the way people assumed things about our family dynamic before even knowing our names.

It wasn't loud. It wasn't always blatant. But it was there. And once I saw it? I couldn't unsee it.

Zadie Ann was five months old when the tape of Ahmaud Arbery being murdered while running was released. I was disgusted and furious. The video seemed very clear, but people were quick to come to the shooter's defense and argue, "We don't know if it was racism or not." People were speaking as if they genuinely didn't believe racism and racial profiling still exist.

I didn't know what to do, but I felt like something had to be said, and this is what I shared in a Facebook post:

> I have been haunted by this tape all day long. So many people believe racism doesn't exist, but I'm here to tell you it does.
>
> You may not think you're racist, but I think if you're white, then, like me, you subconsciously learned there was a hierarchy. It's in the conversations you hear when people say, "I don't have a problem with Black people, but I wouldn't want my daughter to date a Black man."
>
> It's in the subtlety of locking your doors as a Black man walks past your car at the grocery store. It's in the way we assume athleticism and rhythm in all those with darker skin. It's in our churches when our congregations don't accurately reflect our communities. It's in our homes, offices, and businesses when we make assumptions about style, taste, or attitude.
>
> It's everywhere. It's real.
>
> I knew it was bad, but it took having Zadie to realize just how bad it still was.
>
> Can you imagine hearing someone say, "Well, if you waited longer, could you have gotten a white one?"
>
> Can you imagine a close friend being told, "You

know, if I were Kendall and Justin, and I paid that much money, I would have gotten one I wanted."

Can you imagine being asked if your child was from Africa because they clearly couldn't comprehend why a "nice Southern white woman" would adopt a Black baby here in the States?

Can you imagine getting asked if we got a "discount" for adopting a Black baby?

Thankfully, these interactions weren't with family members or close friends but with people we were completely willing to cut out of our lives.

But because of situations like this, among other reasons, Justin and I will forever research the demographic makeup of our neighborhood, schools, and churches.

Black people aren't property. You can't say your daughter can't date a Black guy in high school while wearing a Russell Wilson or Michael Jordan jersey. It's hypocrisy.

SPEAKING UP

A few days after I made that post, I was out strolling through our neighborhood, just like I did most nights.

Our subdivision was massive—well over one hundred homes—and unlike anywhere else I had ever lived, the population was less than 40 percent white.

Every evening as I walked, I saw kids, families, and couples of all colors. They were out barbecuing in their yards, tending to their gardens, shooting hoops, tossing footballs, and more often than not, there was at least one scooter race happening somewhere down the street. It was a beautiful, everyday kind of normal.

But that night, as I passed a Black teenage boy practicing free throws in his driveway, something in me *broke*. My throat tightened, my chest ached, and before I could stop them, the tears started falling *hard*.

Is he scared?

What did his momma have to talk to him about last night after he saw the tape on social media too?

I smiled as I walked by, and Z tried to wave, like she did with everyone those days—blissfully unaware of the weight I was carrying in that moment. I prayed he didn't see the fresh tear on my cheek.

A few moments later, my phone buzzed. Justin had sent me a screenshot of the breaking news—an arrest had been made. A step toward justice for #AhmaudArbery.

The tears kept coming. An ounce of relief in a sea of emotions.

I didn't sleep that night. I cried, holding Zadie Ann,

ashamed of the years I had spent in the bleachers of racism—watching, listening, but never stepping in. But now, standing on the sidelines, it hit so much differently. The disgust I had always felt toward racism was no longer just an abstract moral stance—it was paired with *genuine* heartache and pain.

For years, I had been *silent* on social media. I, too, had scrolled past injustice without sharing articles, without speaking out, because I didn't want to stir up discomfort among the people around me—because I was afraid of how it might affect *my brand*.

But I had learned something gut-wrenching: My silence had spoken volumes to the Black people I called friends. Because the truth was, a *real* friend would have shown up. Would have *spoken* up—not just in private texts, but on Facebook, on Instagram, in meetings, in moments when it *mattered*.

Silence *tells* a story.

Silence as a parent can tell a child this isn't a big deal.

Silence as a Christian can communicate we're pro-life, just not for a grown Black man.

Silence as a friend may say, *I'll speak up only if it happens to you*.

We have to do better. You have to do better. I have to do better.

We must be careful to avoid justifying ignorance and rationalizing bigotry.

COMFORTABLE ISN'T THE GOAL

For many of us, the events of 2020 were the start of our *own* awakening—to the prejudices we had overlooked, ignored, or excused.

But I begged myself: *Don't go back to normal. Don't let this be another tragedy that fades into the background. Challenge your thoughts and tendencies. Challenge the "normal" things around you. Challenge yourself to invest time in the hard conversations*. Because Black people had been fighting this fight for centuries. And it was long past time for my fellow white Christians and me to put our Bibles where our mouths and actions were. It was *our* job to stand in the gap.

We *could* call it what it was.

We *could* flip the table over.

We *had* to.

I *had* to.

Because Zadie Ann *needed* me to.

I tend to be someone who assumes the best in people. I just figured that all Christians were walking around with the same goal: to be more like Christ and to spread his light and love wherever they went. Sure, I know people make mistakes—we *all* fall short—but I thought, at the very least, we were all *trying*. That we shared a heart posture aimed at Jesus.

When I first started posting online, I figured I might get the occasional hate comment. Comes with the territory, right? But over the past five years, I've discovered something that's honestly been pretty unsettling: Mean and harmful comments don't just come from strangers who don't know you, they come from people you know, and people who claim to know Christ.

Yep. You read that right. Maybe you can't believe that or maybe you can because you have also experienced the cliché "There is no hate like Christian love," but if I had a dollar for every time someone left a derogatory, racist, or hateful comment on my content, only to flip over to their profile to see a Bible verse or "Jesus follower" in their biography, I could buy us all a trip to Hawaii.

It is one of the hardest things to reconcile—watching people claim Christ while refusing to acknowledge the prejudice and injustice woven into the world around them. It's painful to see faith reduced to comfort, to hear the same voices that preach love and righteousness fall silent when that love requires action, when that righteousness demands disruption.

But here's the truth: Christianity was never meant to be comfortable. Jesus did not walk this earth to uphold the status quo. He flipped tables, confronted hypocrisy, and made the religious elite deeply uncomfortable. He stood with the oppressed, the marginalized, and the outcast. He didn't just speak about justice—he embodied it. And if we claim to follow him, then we are called to do the same.

As Christians, it is not enough to simply believe in justice in theory. It is not enough to shake our heads in private, to feel sorrow without action, to whisper sympathy but refuse to stand in the fire. Because silence in the face of injustice is not neutrality—it is complicity.

We don't get to choose when our faith applies. We don't get to hold on to Jesus for salvation while ignoring his commands to love our neighbors *fully*, to defend the oppressed, to seek justice and correct oppression (Isaiah 1:17). Faith that refuses to acknowledge injustice is not faith at all—it's self-preservation wrapped in religious rhetoric.

We cannot sit in pews, sing worship songs, and declare ourselves pro-life while turning a blind eye to the very real, very dangerous experiences of Black men, women, and children in America. We cannot claim to love God and yet ignore the cries of his people.

We *must* take up the mantle.

We *must* be the ones who refuse to look away.

We *must* be the ones who speak up, even when it's uncomfortable. Even when it costs us. Even when it disrupts the circles we move in.

Because if our faith is not compelling us to act—if it is not pushing us toward justice, toward advocacy, toward truth—then what, exactly, are we doing?

Jesus did not call us to a passive faith. He did not call us to safe Christianity. He called us to love in radical ways. To defend those who cannot defend themselves. To stand in the gap, to carry the weight, to refuse to be silent in the face of oppression.

And if we, as believers, fail to do that—if we choose comfort over conviction, silence over truth—then we are not following Christ. We are following fear. And that is not a faith I am willing to pass down.

Not to my daughter.

Not to the next generation.

Not ever.

part three

STEWARDING YOUR FLAME

AS I BEGAN WRITING THIS BOOK, I DUSTED off old journals dating back to 2006 and scrolled through fifteen years' worth of social media posts—a time capsule of thoughts, prayers, questions, and half-processed emotions. I knew there were certain moments and memories that needed to be shared, the kind that shaped me, challenged me, and left their mark. But revisiting them wasn't always easy. Some pages felt like looking back at an old friend, familiar and warm, while others felt like walking barefoot over broken glass—sharp, painful, and still capable of drawing blood.

Maybe you've felt that too.

Maybe there are markers in *your* faith journey that you don't revisit lightly. Moments that changed you, for better or worse. Moments when you felt God move so clearly it took your breath away, and others when the silence stretched so long you wondered if he was even listening.

These were the moments when my little fire was being poked, when friction sparked flames that I wasn't sure I could control. There were times the fire raged, refining and illuminating, and times when it flickered so low I thought it might go out entirely. But looking back now, I can see that those were the most transformative moments of my faith. Not the easy ones. Not the peaceful ones. But the ones that forced me to wrestle, to let go, to step deeper into trust.

Because faith is not built in the absence of fire.

It's built in the *heat of it.*

Maybe you're feeling the heat right now. Maybe you're standing in the middle of the fire, working through the friction, trying to make sense of what's left of your faith. Maybe you're sifting through the ashes of old beliefs, wrestling with questions you never thought you'd ask, wondering if what you've always known still holds up under the weight of real life.

If that's you, take a deep breath. You're in the right place.

In this section of the book, I want to walk alongside you as you navigate this refining process. We're going to take a spiritual inventory. We'll start by getting to the core of who you really are, figuring out what season you're in and what you really believe. We'll strip away the noise of culture and expectation to reconsider your identity in Christ—not the version people have told you to be, but the one he's called you to be. And we're going to map out what you actually *believe*—not just what you've inherited, not just what you've always said, but the deep, personal truths that anchor your faith. And yes, we'll also make space for what you're *still* figuring out, because faith is not about having all the answers—it's about holding on even when you don't.

If you're in the fire, know this: You're not alone. And more than that? You're not being consumed. You're being *refined*.

Eight

WHO ARE YOU?

EVER HIT A POINT WHERE YOU DON'T QUITE recognize yourself anymore? Like all the labels, roles, and titles you used to wear just don't seem to fit the same way they used to? And you're sittin' there thinkin', *Who even am I now?* But no matter how long you sit with the question, the answer doesn't come easy.

I've walked through a few seasons like that, but there's one that stands out like it's burned into my memory. It was early April 2016 in the Pacific Northwest, my new home with Justin. After months of gray skies and rain that never seemed to end, my Southern soul was practically *starving* for some sunshine and spring vibes. Back home, April meant azaleas in full bloom, pollen dusting every available surface, and an unspoken rule that pastels and floral prints were the uniform of the season. But I was blissfully unaware that Washington state didn't *celebrate* spring the same way we did back East.

I had been counting down the days until I could pull out my bright colors and Lilly Pulitzer prints, so when we got invited to a function at a local seafood restaurant, I knew *exactly* what I was wearing. I picked out a pink-and-green Lilly skort with crisp white trim, paired it with a white knit top, a woven bag, and my trusty Jack Rogers sandals. It felt *seasonally appropriate*—we were eating on a dock, after all. Sunshine. Water. Fresh seafood. *Springtime perfection.*

Or so I thought.

When we arrived, I stepped into a sea of flannel shirts, jeans, and earth tones as far as the eye could see. Beige, brown, rust, olive green—it was like an REI catalog had exploded in the room. I wish I were exaggerating, but it became *painfully* clear that I had *vastly* underestimated the locals' commitment to looking like they were always prepared for either an impromptu hike or a Nirvana cover band show. There was no in-between.

I, on the other hand, looked like an *Easter egg at a Halloween party.*

It wasn't just that I stood out—it was that I *really* stood out. So much so that at one point someone leaned over and, with genuine curiosity, asked me if I was "dressing up for a certain theme."

A theme? I had to blink a few times before realizing they were *serious*. No, I was not participating in some kind of elaborate costume party. No, this was not a joke. *It was just spring, y'all*. And I thought we were supposed to *dress* like it.

At that moment, homesickness hit me like a freight train. I longed for a place where people understood the value of a vibrant floral print, where "bright and colorful" wasn't a *statement* but just *the norm*. But instead, I was thousands of miles away, standing in a room full of practical, waterproof-jacket-wearing folks who clearly didn't get the memo.

Lesson learned. Spring in Washington might mean blooming cherry blossoms and longer days, but it sure didn't mean breaking out the Lilly Pulitzer.

THE FRICTION OF TRANSITION

If I'm being honest, I was already struggling with my identity in that season, and that evening on the water just quietly confirmed everything I had been feeling but hadn't yet said out loud. I was standing at the intersection of so many changes, caught in the friction of transition, feeling pulled in every direction but not quite sure where I belonged.

I was a recent college grad, a newlywed, and thousands of miles away from everything I had ever known. And let me tell you—those miles might as well have been *light-years*.

Not long before, I had been juggling the full, vibrant chaos of my college life: sorority president, triple major, photography-business owner, always running from one thing to the next with a sense of purpose and a massive village of people I could call at a moment's notice. I had *built* something for myself, carved out an identity that was mine and mine alone, and I wore every one of those titles like badges of honor.

And then, seemingly overnight, I wasn't any of those things anymore.

I was *somebody's stay-at-home wife.*

My emergency contact was a fellow military wife I had met *exactly once.*

I was in a world where nobody cared about my GPA, my leadership roles, or the business I had built from the ground up. Instead, I was simply known as *Lieutenant Dunn's wife.*

And it was *a lot* to process.

It wasn't that I wasn't proud of Justin or the life we were building together—I *was.* But going from being someone with a name and accomplishments of my own to suddenly feeling like I had been absorbed into someone else's identity?

That was a hard pill to swallow. I had never felt smaller and yet somehow *completely invisible* all at the same time.

During this season, I was also battling health challenges—ones that I had shoved to the back burner for a while but were now demanding my full attention. And with that came an internal war I never saw coming.

See, for as long as I could remember, I had confidently said—*and truly believed*—that I never wanted biological children. It wasn't that I didn't want to be a mother. I absolutely did. But I had always felt called to adoption. That was the plan, the vision, the thing I spoke about with certainty whenever the topic came up.

But then, suddenly, that decision wasn't *mine* to make anymore.

Doctors started throwing around words like *infertility* and *options* and *not likely*, and I felt something shift inside me. Because even though I had never planned on carrying a child, now that I was being told I might not even have the choice, something in me started pushing back.

It was like a stubborn part of my soul stood up and crossed its arms, determined to prove them wrong.

I wrestled with emotions I didn't know how to name. It was confusing and frustrating, grappling with the fact that I had spent years believing one thing about myself, only to feel something entirely different when the decision was no longer in my hands.

Was it grief? Was it defiance? Was it my body's way of reacting to the sudden realization that what I once saw as my choice was now something I might never get to experience, even if I *wanted* to?

I didn't know.

All I knew was that the certainty I once had didn't feel so certain anymore. And to make it even harder, I was constantly surrounded by other wives my age who were announcing pregnancies, decorating nurseries, and swapping baby name ideas over brunch. I smiled and congratulated them—because I *was* happy for them—but deep down, I felt alone in a way I had never experienced before.

It wasn't just a physical separation from the life I had known; it was an invisible separation from the timeline my peers were still comfortably moving along—the one I had been forcibly pushed off of. They were walking a path I had always assumed I *chose* not to take, but now I wasn't even sure if I had the option. It was a strange kind of grief—grieving something I had never thought I wanted, yet suddenly feeling the loss of it as if it had been ripped away.

And as if that wasn't enough, my body had become a battleground too. Between my health diagnoses, the medications, and the weight of stress pressing down on me, I had gained forty pounds in just a few short months. When I looked in the mirror, I didn't even recognize myself.

My clothes didn't fit. My face looked fuller. I saw pictures of myself and barely even recognized the girl staring back. And it wasn't just about the weight—it was the *disconnect.* I felt like I was losing myself in every possible way.

I was in a full-blown identity crisis.

Physically, emotionally, spiritually—every piece of me felt *foreign.* Like I had somehow become a stranger to my own life, stuck in a body I didn't recognize, living in a place that didn't feel like home, watching everyone around me move forward while I stood there, trying to figure out where I even belonged.

Justin and I were also broke newlyweds, with only one car, and though my photography and design businesses were going well, I still had a lot of time on my hands, certainly more than I was used to. After completing my work and straightening up our tiny 400-square-foot apartment, I was left bored and frustrated with myself. I quickly learned that when you are in an identity crisis like this, you don't even like the company of yourself because you no longer relate to who you thought you were.

And on top of all of those things, one of the main ways that I had always identified myself as—a Good Christian Girl—was also going through changes. I had begun working through some big questions and inconsistencies in my faith in college, but Jesus was still the person I ran to. My faith, my relationship with Christ, was the only thing that carried over, but it began to shift too. Growing up, I had heard plenty of talks and sermons about keeping your identity in Christ, and to me, that meant making sure I kept my identity as a Christian as a top priority. I needed to look, act, and believe like a good Christian at all times.

But when your good Christian identity is falling apart and seemingly doesn't translate in a new season, you're left to realize that being a "good Christian" can be really shallow and act as a facade. I now like to call it "Hobby Lobby faith": Like the pretty painted signs that say "Have Faith" or "With God All Things Are Possible" written in a pretty script font on a distressed shiplap canvas, it looks good from the outside, but it is more decorative than life steering. There is not a lot of depth to it.

I needed to get my life together and figure out who I was in this chapter, and my Hobby Lobby faith was no longer going to cut it. I began reading the Bible in search of answers, but it only made me have more questions. However, these questions weren't the kind of questions that were connected to doubt; this time, they involved excitement and curiosity. I wanted to understand the context and the how and why between the verses. I got my first adult study Bible where the margins are filled with footnotes and extra information and I was drinking it up, in a desperate search for more.

As empty and broken as I felt, there was an uncanny pattern I could see developing. The more I read and studied, the less all those worries and problems consumed me. It was the first time I had read the Bible for myself without the direction of a teacher or leader or the accompaniment of a Bible study or devotional. I was beginning to figure out there was so much more to it than what I had been carefully fed as a child and adolescent.

For the first time, I didn't just read the Bible because someone told me to. I didn't just follow a devotional or sit in a study where the conclusions were already drawn for me. I *searched*. I dug. I questioned—not out of doubt, but out of a hunger to know what had been there all along.

And what I found was life changing.

My identity in Christ wasn't about performance. It wasn't about upholding a Christian reputation or staying within the lines of cultural Christianity. It wasn't about how well I followed a checklist of spiritual dos and don'ts.

It was about *who God says I am*.

It was about a faith strong enough to sustain me when the labels and roles I had clung to were stripped away. A faith that wasn't built on *appearance* but on *actual relationship*.

Because if our identity in Christ is only as strong as our ability to keep up a good-Christian facade, then we don't have faith—we have *a brand*. And that kind of faith will never carry us through the seasons that break us open and force us to rebuild.

But when we dig deeper—when we seek him *for ourselves*, when we let Scripture shape us instead of settling for what Christian culture tells us to be—we find something *real*.

Something *solid*.

Something that doesn't just look good hanging on the wall but actually holds us up when everything else falls away.

And that's the kind of faith I wanted. The kind of faith that wasn't just *for show* but for *life*.

HOW TO GROUND YOUR IDENTITY IN CHRIST

If you are sitting there feeling like you are in your own identity crisis or maybe just not sure where to even start with reclaiming your faith and identity, I have a few little exercises I want you to try:

1. Rewrite your conversations with God.

Most of us have been taught that prayer should sound a certain way—polished, structured, and formal. But real prayer is about *relationship*, not performance.

Exercise

- Set a timer for five minutes and write out a prayer as if you were talking to a close friend. No filters, no fancy words—just *honesty*.
- Don't hold back. If you're frustrated, say it. If you have questions, ask them. If you don't know what to say, tell him that too.
- If writing isn't your thing, voice-record yourself praying or go on a prayer walk and talk out loud, or in your head, as you go.

Reflection

- How did this feel different from your usual prayers?
- Did you feel freer? More connected? More real?
- Make this a habit. Keep a journal of your unfiltered prayers and look back to see how God meets you in them over time.

2. Dismantle the "Hobby Lobby faith."

Sometimes we shape our identity in Christ based on what Christian culture tells us instead of what *God actually says* in Scripture. This can lead to a shallow faith that looks good on the surface but doesn't sustain us in hard seasons.

Exercise:

- Grab a journal and divide a page into two columns:
  - Left column: Write down statements or beliefs you've been taught about your identity as a Christian (for example, "Good Christians don't struggle with doubt"; "God is disappointed in me when I mess up and miss the mark"; "If I do everything right, God will bless me").
  - Right column: Find scriptures that actually define your identity in Christ (for example, Ephesians 2:10 says we are God's handiwork; Romans 8:1 says there is no condemnation for those in Christ; Isaiah 43:1 says we are called by name and belong to him).
- Compare the two lists. Which beliefs align with God's Word? Which ones need to be unlearned?

Reflection

- How much of your identity has been shaped by church culture versus Scripture?
- Looking at the words you used to describe yourself, do they bring up more negative or positive feelings and connotations? Where do you think those labels and words came from? Where did those feelings and beliefs start in your own life?
- How does knowing who God says you are change how you see yourself?

For me, this is where I constantly have to do the work to rewire the way I view my body, not through a lens of shame as we talked about before.

3. Find God in your everyday life.

One of the biggest revelations in the passage above was realizing that God meets us *exactly where we are*—not just in church, but in the car, the kitchen, the mundane moments of life.

Exercise

- Over the next week, intentionally invite God into your daily routine:
  - Talk to him while doing dishes.
  - Pray in the shower.
  - Listen for him while driving.
  - Read one verse before checking social media in the morning.
- Write down moments when you felt his presence or guidance—even in small, unexpected ways.

Reflection

- How did acknowledging God in the *ordinary* change the way you connected with him?
- Did this practice help you realize that your relationship with God isn't limited to church, devotionals, or "spiritual" activities?

Finding your identity in Christ isn't about *performing faith*—it's about living in relationship with him. That means coming as you are, breaking free from shallow or cultural Christianity, and letting him meet you in the *real*, everyday moments of life.

Give these exercises a try and see if your sense of who you are in Christ starts to feel less like a pretty idea hanging on the wall and more like something rooted, real, and life-giving—something that sinks down deep and actually shapes the way you live.

Nine

WHAT SEASON ARE YOU IN?

HAVE YOU EVER GONE TO A BOOT CAMP–STYLE workout class? You know, the ones that are at the crack of dawn and five days a week? Unfortunately, I had the bright idea of signing up for one of these in college. I'm sure I was motivated by spring break or whatever early 2010s diet of the moment, but I couldn't tell you my exact rationale for signing up. However, I can tell you what happened on that first day. It was called the "Physical Assessment."

My instructor told us, "We are going to see where you are at, so we can find out where you need to go." I wasn't aware we were going anywhere. Matter of fact, I was questioning why I had shown up there at that moment. He had a series of different pieces of equipment and stations we were going to work through before ending with a timed run. At the time, I thought the only purpose of the assessment was to see how much stronger or faster we got over the course of the class, but by the end I realized the assessment was a tool to see what kind of exercises would actually help me—not just what looked impressive or hard, but what targeted the right muscles and imbalances. It wasn't about judgment; it was about awareness.

And honestly? That's what taking a *spiritual inventory* feels like.

It's not just about tracking your growth or proving how "strong" your faith is—it's focused on getting honest about where you are so you can begin to heal, stretch, and strengthen the parts of your soul that actually need it. It's about pausing long enough to ask: *Where am I spiritually? What's weighing me down? What have I been carrying that God never asked me to?*

Because just like our bodies, our faith journeys need regular check-ins—not to shame us, but to guide us. Let's start this journey the way you would any good road trip, by thinking about the playlist.

WHAT'S YOUR SONG?

It's crazy how music has this way of capturing emotions we can't quite put into words—how a single song can pull something out of us that we didn't even realize was buried. I think sometimes we're so good at putting on a strong or brave face, at compartmentalizing and pushing forward, that we don't even *know* how we really feel.

But music?

Music has a way of telling the truth for us.

Just ask any teenager in the late 2000s who *carefully* picked their Myspace song to send a *very specific* message to their entire friend group. Those weren't just songs; they were *statements.* Or remember making mix CDs, labeling them with Sharpies, curating the perfect track list for every occasion? *Hype Playlist. Slow Jamzzz.* I even had one called *Hate Music for Broken Hearts*—because sometimes teenage angst needs a soundtrack.

What a time to be alive.

But I think you get my point. Music plays an integral role in our lives, and our spiritual life is no exception.

Here's something to think about: If this season of your life had a theme song, what would it be?

I have this habit: I'll latch on to a song and play it *out*, over and over, until everyone around me is ready to throw my phone out the window. But I can't let go. It's like I need to soak it in, let it settle into my bones until it becomes part of me.

When we were waiting during the adoption process, it was "Faithful" by Elevation Worship, a song that became the background track to my waiting, my hoping, my trusting. The next summer it was "Million Dollar Baby" by Tommy Richman—blasting in the kitchen, feet moving, heart light, those moments when life felt full and easy.

Music has a way of affecting us. It can pump you up, flood you with good vibes, or wrap around you like a warm blanket in the middle of a storm.

And right now? Right now I need something to hold on to. We're just days away from another deployment, and all our plans for the year have been flipped upside down. It's the kind of unexpected turn that leaves you reeling, trying to steady yourself even as the ground keeps shifting beneath you.

The deployment news hit *at the exact same time* as another blow—finding out that the medications Justin had been taking to help with fertility weren't working.

For years, we've held on to hope, trying, waiting, believing that one day the pieces would finally fall into place. We had decided that 2025 would be our *last* effort to get pregnant before moving forward with a hysterectomy and fully shifting our focus to adoption again—something we planned to do either way.

We really thought *this* would be the year. The year of answers. The year of forward motion. The year of *finally*.

And now? Now it feels impossible. Like trying to hold on to something that keeps slipping through my fingers.

Like praying prayers that feel unheard. Like standing at yet another crossroads, wondering which way we're supposed to go.

I don't know how this story plays out yet. But what I *do* know is that somehow, through all of it—through waiting, through disappointment, through plans unraveling and new ones being made—there's always been a song to carry me through.

When I first heard "Hard Fought Hallelujah" by Brandon Lake, it was the Godwink I didn't know I needed. Every lyric, every theme ran parallel to the heart of this book—this idea that faith isn't always neat and tidy, that sometimes it's scraped together from the ashes, held together by sheer will, wrestled into existence in the middle of life's hardest moments.

Then when the new version with Jelly Roll dropped? It hit *different*. Something about his voice makes me emotional in a way I can't quite explain. It's raw, unpolished in the best way, full of grit and heartbreak and hard-earned redemption. You don't just *hear* him sing it—you *feel* it. Like he isn't just performing a song; he's *living* it.

It's the kind of voice that carries the weight of someone who's been there—someone who knows what it's like to plead with God on a cold bathroom floor, to sit in the sterile quiet of a doctor's office, to fight for faith when it would be easier to walk away.

And maybe that's why it hits so hard. Because faith like that? It's not *pretty*. It's not polished or perfect or effortlessly confident. It's a *hard-fought hallelujah*. The kind you claw your way to. The kind that costs you something. The kind that means *more* because you know exactly what it took to get there.

What song are you playing on repeat right now?

And listen—this isn't about picking a "church answer" or forcing a deep spiritual meaning where there isn't one. There's *no* right answer. But I do believe music can serve as a *diagnostic tool*, giving us insight into where we are emotionally, mentally, and spiritually.

Because most of us use music like a *thermometer* for our mood—whether we realize it or not. We instinctively reach for certain songs depending on how we feel. We play different music on a long road trip than the kind we play after a breakup. The songs we blast during a kitchen dance party aren't the same ones we listen to when we're unwinding in bed or soaking in the tub after a long day.

Music *sets the tone*, but it also becomes the *backdrop*—a reflection of where we are, what we're feeling, and maybe even what we *need* to feel.

Take a second. Think about it.

What's your theme song right now? What playlist are you listening to?

Now that you've had a little time to think about it, where did you land?

What song is capturing this season for you?

If you're able to right now, grab a piece of paper, and let's take it *old school* with a bubble brainstorm.

Step 1: Write the name of your song in the middle of the paper.

Big, bold, front and center. This is *your* song right now—the one that's resonating with you, whether you fully understand why yet or not.

Step 2: Start brainstorming around it.

Draw little lines branching out from the song title and jot down words, thoughts, or feelings that come up. Here are a few prompts to get you going:

- *What is the tempo of the song like?* Is it slow and reflective? Upbeat and energetic? Does it build gradually or stay steady throughout?
- *What genre would this song fall into?* Is it a soulful ballad? A country anthem? A rock song that makes you want to roll the windows down and feel something?

- *What is the song's mood or emotional tone?* Try to list three to five words that describe how the song feels. Is it hopeful? Melancholy? Determined? Nostalgic?
- *What are the lyrics about?* Without overthinking, jot down the themes that stand out to you. Is it about resilience? Love? Loss? Celebration? A new beginning?

Step 3: Look at what you've written.

Grab a highlighter and highlight any of the words and descriptors that also describe how you are feeling and what season you are in.

Step back and ask yourself, *Does anything surprise me? What do these words reveal about where I am right now?* Just like in art history all those years ago, I have learned to analyze everything a bit deeper and see that there is so much more than meets your eye or ear the first time.

This is more than just a fun exercise—it's a way to check in with yourself. Because sometimes we don't fully recognize what we're feeling until we see it staring back at us in black and white. For me? It helps separate me from my emotions so I can truly assess them, and it's a great way to check in with myself.

Take your time. Write it out. See what unfolds.

SPIRITUAL INVENTORY

Now that we've peeled back a few emotional layers and gotten a little more in touch with how we're *really* feeling, let's take it a step further. I want you to consider where you are on a spiritual level—not where you *think* you should be, not where you *wish* you were, but where you *actually* are.

And let's be clear—this isn't about guilt or shame. This isn't about feeling like you should have it all together or pretending you don't have questions. It's about *awareness. Growth.* Getting real with yourself and with God about what's working, what's not, and where you might need to recalibrate.

Here's the deal: *There's no right or wrong answer.* This isn't a test, and I'm not handing out report cards. Just a good old-fashioned gut check. Grab some coffee—or sweet tea if that's your thing—get comfy, and let's get real about where we're at.

- If I had to sum up my faith in this season with just one word, what would it be? Be honest. If it's fried, frazzled, or figuring it out, or if it's completely nonexistent, that's okay too.
- Do I feel like God and I are thick as thieves right now, or does it seem like he's a little hard to reach?

Or somewhere in between, like that one friend who takes three to five business days to text back?

- Have I been showing up for my spiritual life—praying, worshiping, reading Scripture—or has it felt more like trying to start a cold car on a winter morning?
- What emotions have been most tied to my faith lately: peace, doubt, hope, frustration, apathy?

Let's go one step further and reflect on the moments, challenges, and experiences that have played a role in your life.

- *What life experiences have stretched, shaken, or straight-up tested my faith the most?* Think of the moments that made you whisper, *All right, God, what exactly are we doing here?*
- *When was the last time I felt like God* really *saw me—not just in a general, Sunday-school-answer kind of way, but in a deep, personal,* "That was for me" *kind of way?*
- *Have there been moments when I've looked back and thought, Yep, that was definitely God, even if I couldn't see it at the time?*
- *When life gets hard, do I run* toward *God, white-knuckling my faith, or do I start avoiding him like an unread text I just don't have the energy to open?*

Once you have gotten your answers down, let's see where you are.

If you've never done much "self-work"—never sat with a journal, never processed things out loud, never spent time with a therapist—exercises like this might feel a little silly at first. Maybe even unnecessary. But here's the thing: There's something *powerful* about putting thoughts into words and getting them out of your head and onto paper. It forces you to organize the tangled mess of emotions instead of just letting them bounce around in your brain like a rogue bouncy ball in a small room. Thoughts can be slippery when they stay internal, but writing them down? That's where clarity starts to take shape.

Now that you've scribbled or typed out your answers, let's take a step back and look at what's in front of you. I'm going to take a *wild* guess here, but if you're reading this book, you're probably feeling *some type of way*—and I'm betting it's not all rainbows, sunshine, and a perfect cup of coffee on a slow Saturday morning.

Maybe your words look a little like this: *lonely, frustrated, overwhelmed, exhausted, sad*. Maybe they feel a little heavier than you expected. And if that's the case, *I see you*.

If we're being honest, however, we *all* feel a tinge

of those emotions at one point or another. It's part of being human. But when you're wrestling with *faith*—the very thing that's *supposed* to bring you joy, comfort, and direction—those emotions can feel even heavier. Because when faith starts feeling hard, it's easy to wonder, *What's wrong with me? Why does this feel so heavy? Why isn't this working like it used to?*

But here's what I need you to hear: *There is nothing wrong with you*. Faith isn't *always* light and easy. Sometimes it's a battle. Sometimes it's built in the tension. And sometimes the fact that you're feeling the weight of it all is just proof that your faith is *alive*—that it *matters*.

So, take a breath. You're not alone in this. Let's keep going.

Ten

WHO IS IN YOUR VILLAGE?

"YOU CAN ALWAYS COME HOME." IT was a silent but known principle at my parents' house. Whether it was calling at 11:30 p.m. homesick at a sleepover, a semester into college at a school that didn't quite fit, or having a hard time while Justin was gone for training—I always knew I could go home.

Home wasn't just my parents' log cabin outside our small town, and it wasn't just my parents. Going home meant going back to my community. It was a familiar routine, familiar faces, and people I could count on if I were to need anything, big or small.

A vital part of that community for me has always been my church family. The people I ate Wednesday night dinners with, the adults who poured into me as a kid for Sunday school, the ladies who brought food over when someone was sick, and the friends who sent texts "checking in."

When I think of my home church and my community, the words that come to mind are "safe" and "comfortable." Even though I have walked through difficult seasons with church, walking into the sanctuary and seeing our stained-glass windows still fills me with relief and contentment; the church I grew up in has always felt like home.

I truly believe that it was because I had such a rock-solid foundation in my faith and a strong community that I was able to walk through difficult seasons of doubt, frustration, and questions without completely losing my footing. It wasn't that I never struggled—it was that even when I did, I *knew* what I was holding on to.

But I've come to realize that not everyone has that same experience.

For me, church was a place of warmth, community, and belonging. It was where I learned about God's love, where I built friendships, where I found security in something bigger than myself. Even when I faced hard questions, I never felt like my faith was *fragile*—it was woven into the fabric of my life, something I could lean on when things got shaky.

But for my husband, church wasn't that way at all.

We grew up in the same area, but his experience with faith was vastly different from mine. Where I had memories of Vacation Bible School, church potlucks, and youth group lock-ins, his memories were laced with obligation, discomfort, and a growing sense of disillusionment. Church wasn't a place of deep relationships or personal growth—it was just something he had to sit through. He went because he was expected to, not because he felt drawn to it. And as he got older, he wasn't sure if he even *believed* any of it.

It wasn't until I got to college that I realized his story wasn't the exception—it was the norm for many people.

Here I was, attending a private Christian university, surrounded by students I assumed had grown up with experiences similar to mine. But instead of shared excitement and confidence in their faith, I kept hearing the same heartbreaking theme: stories of church hurt, of legalism, of feeling unheard, unseen, or unworthy in the very place that was supposed to bring healing.

Some had grown up in environments where faith was reduced to a rigid set of rules—an exhausting checklist of dos and don'ts with little grace for mistakes. Others had witnessed hypocrisy firsthand—church leaders who preached about love and kindness but showed judgment and exclusion. Some had been part of communities where hard questions weren't welcomed, where doubt was treated as rebellion, where wrestling with faith meant you were on dangerous ground.

And many of them? They had walked away from faith altogether—not because they didn't *want* to believe, but because they had never been given a safe space to work through their questions.

I started to realize that while my faith had been built on love, grace, and genuine relationship, many others had been handed a version of faith that felt conditional, fragile, or even harmful.

And that wrecked me.

Because faith was never supposed to be *just* a routine. It was never supposed to be a set of rules or a Sunday performance. It was meant to be real, transformative, life-giving. But when churches fail to reflect the heart of God—when they prioritize image over authenticity, control over compassion, or rules over relationship—they don't just push people away from church. They push people away from Jesus himself. And that is something we cannot afford to ignore.

So, what do you do if church doesn't feel like home? What if church has a lot of hard feelings attached? What if you have never stepped foot in church because of the fear of being an outsider trying to fit in?

REAL RELATIONSHIPS

There's one common thread that weaves through all my stories—through the seasons of doubt, the times I felt distant from God, and the thousands of questions I've carried: There has always been *community*. The people around me who waded into the deep waters, who sat with me in silence, and who helped me work through the questions, even if they didn't have all the answers.

I believe that being part of a community meets two very real needs we all have:

- Meaningful relationships
- A supportive village

The value of community lies in real relationship connections—not the superficial kind we see on LinkedIn, or the parasocial ones we form online. I'm talking about the kind of relationships that go beyond surface-level conversations and awkward small talk in the grocery store aisle. We need meaningful bonds with people we care about—and who genuinely care about us.

These kinds of relationships come with many names: friendships, mentorships, discipleships, even romantic relationships. I like to call them mutual "ships"—the kind that bring value, intimacy, and connection. We all need people who cheer us on when we win, who don't see us as competition, and who believe in us when we take big, bold steps. And just as importantly, we need people who sit with us in our doubt, acknowledge our pain, and hold our hands through heartbreak and disappointment.

A few years ago I learned about the Jewish practice of *sitting shiva*. *Shiva* is the Hebrew word for seven, and the practice involves sitting with someone who is grieving for seven days following a loss. The goal isn't to fix or speak—it's simply to *be* with them in their grief. To sit quietly beside them, low to the ground, offering presence instead of solutions.

We see this in the Bible, in Job chapter 2. After Job experienced great loss, three of his friends came to sit shiva with him. Verse 13 says, "They sat with him on the ground seven days and seven nights, and no one spoke a word to him, for they saw that his suffering was very great" (ESV).

What a beautiful picture of friendship. No need for eloquent words, the perfect gift, or doing the "right" thing. Just being near—*that* was enough.

A few weeks ago I experienced what I've come to call an "episode." The doctors aren't quite sure what to make of them yet, but I've had enough to recognize the patterns when one is coming on. It's not exactly like a panic attack. I've had those, too, but it's something similar.

It usually starts with a heaviness in my body—like I can suddenly feel the weight of every single pound I'm made of. Then a tingling sensation creeps into my hands as my mind begins to race, and I'm hit with that full-body fight-or-flight response, like something is physically chasing me . . . even though I'm just lying in bed. That's when I know: I need to call for backup.

My husband is always my first call, followed by my mom. But when neither of them could get to me in time, I called my dad. He heard the panic in my voice—choppy and tearful—and said, "I'm on the way."

I stood up to go to the bathroom, afraid I was about to get sick. And if I throw up once, I can guarantee it's going to happen another dozen times. As I stood there, adrenaline surging and my brain trying to convince me I needed to run or hide, my legs started to feel numb. That's when I heard my dad coming up the stairs.

He walked in, eyes wide, and asked, "What do I need to do? Do you need medicine? Something to eat? Are you about to pass out?" Bless his heart, he had never seen me like that, and it was clear he didn't know what to make of it. If my mom or Justin were there, they'd know the drill. But my dad? He was clueless.

I told him, "I just need you to stand here with me. Tell me nothing's wrong, that no one's after me. And if I throw up, just put a cold compress on my neck."

He looked at me like I'd just handed him the strangest set of marching orders. I mean, what do you *do* when someone says they don't really need you to *do* anything?

That's the strange thing about these episodes. They come in like waves, and whether I like it or not, one's going to crash. I just need someone to stand in it with me. I've tried medications before. Breathing exercises help a little. But there's something powerful about having someone *be there*. It's like my body starts to calibrate to theirs. Seeing that they're okay, hearing that *I'm* okay—that's often enough to convince my subconscious there's no bear, no intruder, no real threat at all.

THE VILLAGE

When I hear the phrase "the village," my brain immediately flashes to a picture of small houses lined along a dirt road, leading to a little market square—something out of the pioneering days. I'm not sure why exactly, but in my mind, there are chickens roaming free, horses tied to posts, and barefoot kids running around in the dust. Maybe it's an image left over from some old social studies textbook I read two decades ago, but whatever it is, it's what the word *village* stirs up for me.

Villages aren't just a concept from the past, though. But somewhere along the way, I think we've strayed pretty far from that model. Most people don't know the names of their neighbors anymore, much less make a habit of borrowing sugar or eggs. We no longer live in a society that revolves around the collective good. Instead, we operate much more individually.

I mean, really—why do we all own lawn mowers?

Every single house on the street has one, even though we're not all mowing at the same time. And you certainly won't catch *me* mowing at 7:00 a.m. Wouldn't it be amazing if you shared a lawnmower with a couple of your neighbors? I think that's just one tiny example of how disconnected we've become. We've moved away from a way of life that was once so beautifully intertwined.

How can we expect to sit and ask difficult theological or personal questions when we no longer feel comfortable asking our neighbors for a cup of sugar or to borrow their leaf blower? Now, I am not going to sit here and try to act like I have the remedy for living in an increasingly individualist culture, but I can share with you how I have found it possible to cultivate a safe place to ask questions and grow vulnerably in faith.

WHERE TWO OR MORE ARE GATHERED

If walking into a church feels too heavy or plain impossible right now, can I just tell you, there's something sacred about pulling up a chair with just one other person. Faith doesn't have to be built in stained-glass sanctuaries or polished pews. Sometimes it grows best in the smallest, quietest gatherings—in living rooms, coffee shops, or the front seat of a car.

The Bible says in Matthew 18:20, "For where two or three gather in my name, there am I with them." Jesus was talking to his disciples about what life together as believers ought to look like. And isn't it comforting? He's not asking for a crowd—just a few hearts willing to lean in.

Now don't get me wrong, I believe God meets us when we're alone too. Sitting with your Bible, journaling your prayers, or just reflecting on what he's doing in your life . . . those moments are vital. But there's a different kind of holy ground when you're knee to knee with someone else, both of you hungry to learn and grow.

Some of my most defining faith moments didn't happen under a steeple. They happened riding shotgun with a friend, talking out the hard questions about God, grace, and what it means to live this out. It wasn't fancy or formal. But it was real—and it changed me.

You don't need a friend who lines up with you on every single belief or agrees with you on all the fine-print details of theology. What matters more is finding someone who's willing to have honest conversations—someone who doesn't just nod politely at your questions but leans in and helps you search for the answers. It's not about matching theology; it's about matching heart postures.

Two people with humble spirits and a shared hunger to look a little more like Jesus every day—that's what a safe place to grow in faith really looks like.

IF YOU CAN'T FIND IT, CREATE IT

Throughout my life, whenever I was looking for a specific opportunity or community and couldn't quite put my finger on it, my mom would remind me, "Well, Kendall, maybe this just means it's your job to do it." This could apply to a club in school or a business idea, but it also applied to faith community.

In 2016, when I was coming out of my really dark season, fresh off a nervous breakdown, living across the country from my support system, and looking in the mirror at a body I didn't recognize, I was desperate to be able to talk about what I was experiencing through the lens of faith. But at that point, you would be hard-pressed to find anyone talking about mental health, infertility, and cultural differences in a faith-based setting. You can't tie up depression with a cute bow at the end of a sermon, and infertility was often pushed aside as a simple prayer request. I felt frustrated and alone because I knew I couldn't be the only one going through these things and I knew my feelings mattered to God.

What did I do? I started writing, I started blogging my experiences of living with both faith and anxiety. I began openly talking about our struggles with infertility and belief that God was working in the situation, but how I was still holding space for the grief we were experiencing. And do you know what happened? People responded. There was a number of women who were experiencing the same things I was; they were also living in the juxtaposition of faith and questions and were looking for a place to dive deeper into faith and talk about the parts of life that had felt taboo or off limits in more traditional faith settings.

Maybe that's where you are right now—longing for a place where you can wrestle with your faith and your real-life struggles without fear of judgment. A space where your questions aren't shushed or brushed aside but welcomed as part of the journey.

If you can't seem to find that space, can I gently suggest that maybe it's yours to create? Maybe God has placed that longing in your heart because he wants you to be the one to go first. It doesn't have to be a big production. You don't need a platform or a perfectly curated Bible study plan. You just need a willing heart and a little bit of courage to say, "Hey, can we talk about this?"

Text a friend. Invite her for coffee. Sit across from each other at the kitchen table or in the front seat of your car. Bring your questions. Bring your doubts. Bring your hope. And watch how God shows up in those simple, sacred conversations.

Because here's the thing: You don't have to have all the answers to create a safe place for faith to grow. You just have to show up—and invite someone else to do the same.

Eleven

WHAT DO YOU REALLY BELIEVE AND WHY?

IN COLLEGE, ONE QUESTION CRACKED OPEN everything I thought I knew about faith: What do I *really* believe? Not *what have I been told* to believe. Not *what have I inherited* from my upbringing, my church, or the people around me. But what do I actually know to be true? Do I hold on to certain beliefs simply because they were presented as *rules*—because someone in authority told me "That's just the way it is" and I never thought to question it? Or do I believe what I believe because I've done the work of seeking it out—because I've dug into Scripture, wrestled with it, measured it against Christ's character, and seen the evidence of God's truth in my own life?

I can pinpoint the exact instance when I first confronted this question. I was sitting in chapel on Wednesday morning my sophomore year of college. With my mind on classes and an upcoming Greek-life meeting, I was not prepared to intervene for a stranger, but that's what ended up happening.

I knew the name and major of the girl sitting next to me in chapel, but I didn't *know* her. We were simply predestined by the college to sit next to each other in chapel for the semester, and our relationship had gone no deeper than small talk as we listened to the special guests and chapel speakers. But on that day there wasn't a speech to listen to or a nonprofit cause to learn about. Instead, we were having a group discussion on the intersection of church and culture. There was a moderator, but her job was simply to supply the questions, and the student ministers would run microphones around the one-thousand-person auditorium.

The first questions were nothing too serious, but the conversation took a quick turn when the moderator asked, "What do you think is the biggest problem facing the church today?"

It was a broad question, with lots of possibility. One student in the audience quickly raised his hand. He took the mic and said, "It's the homosexuals. It's because of them that this country is going to hell in a handbasket, and we're going to become the next Sodom and Gomorrah."

There were a couple of gasps but also a wave of amens.

I realized the girl next to me was crying. Not a few emotional tears, but full-on sobs. I had heard homosexuality was a sin from the pulpit before, but the way it was being talked about in this chapel—the words used and the vehemence behind those words—wasn't sitting right with me.

Without thinking, my hand shot into the air. *Jesus, give me the words*, I prayed. I didn't have an agenda; I wasn't even sure I had an answer. I just knew that the girl beside me needed a friend and she needed Jesus, and in that moment, I could at least try to be a voice of love.

The student minister handed me the mic, and I stood. "It's easy to point fingers at other people," I said. "But I think the biggest problem facing the church today is that people are more concerned with how other people are doing Christianity than with trying to actually look like Jesus."

The young woman beside me was still leaning into her hands as I gave back the mic and sat down. I knew my words weren't going to fix anything, but I needed her to know I saw her and her pain. I turned to her and asked if she was okay. She told me she had just come out to her parents and was hurt by their response. "I'm sorry," I told her. "I am so sorry." We grabbed our bags as the dismissal chimed.

I felt the familiar feeling of tears and friction come through my body, and my head was spinning. I left with questions like *Why was I having such a strong, almost physical reaction as I sat there?* And *If Jesus stood in the gap for people, why were so many people so quick to place blame and hurt other people? How could people who claim love and grace make someone feel so broken?*

As I thought about that chapel over the next few days, weeks, and months, I realized that my faith up to that point had led me to believe that the world was black and white. I thought that I would always be able to clearly recognize what was Christian and what wasn't. But in those moments during chapel, nothing felt clear. Up until that point, I'd felt so sure of so many of things, but truthfully, that certainty was built on the words of other people and hypotheticals I had never had to face or wrestle with instead of being built on my relationship with Jesus. But seeing the way another Christian's words had affected the girl next to me made me want to examine what I really believed about everything related to my faith and how I lived my life as a Christian.

I believed that Christ was good—not just good, but the very embodiment of love, grace, and justice. I believed that he called us to *do* good, to love selflessly, to care for the marginalized and walk humbly. But if that were true, then why did so many Christians seem to do so much harm? Why did some of the same people who claimed to follow Jesus use faith as a weapon instead of a refuge? Why did the church—supposed to be a place of healing—so often feel like a place of wounding?

I thought back to how I had felt after Justin's mom's death and how some people in the church talked about suicide and how it made me feel. And I started to notice how sometimes the poor, the grieving, the misunderstood were marginalized in a way that didn't reflect Jesus.

These were the questions that haunted me—not because I wanted to walk away from faith, but because I wanted to understand it. To strip away the layers of human influence, cultural traditions, and legalistic expectations and get back to the *heart* of what Jesus actually called us to. And that's when the Holy Spirit came in and kept pointing me back to Scripture and the life of Jesus.

Because if we claim to follow him, but our faith doesn't look like him—if it doesn't reflect his love, his mercy, his radical grace—then who are we following? Maybe it's less about having every right answer, and more about following the right person.

WHO ARE YOU FOLLOWING?

I wish I could tell you that I have it all figured out. I wish I could wrap up the book with a bow knowing that I had it all figured out and had happily passed it on to you, but I don't. But what I do have are some questions and prompts that I have asked myself and continue to ask myself to help me work through, dig deeper, and process the more difficult seasons of faith.

I hope you will grab a journal and use them to help you wherever you are with your faith:

1. What do I actually believe about God, Jesus, and faith—and why?

- Is this something I believe because I've experienced it firsthand, or is it something I was simply taught?
- Have I ever taken the time to study and wrestle with these beliefs on my own?
- If no one had ever told me what to believe, what conclusions would I have come to?
- What does the Bible actually have to say about this?

2. Where do my beliefs come from—Scripture, tradition, or cultural Christianity?

- Have I searched the Bible for myself to see what it actually says, or have I accepted only what I've been told?
- Do my beliefs align with the character of Jesus as shown in Scripture?
- Are my beliefs tied to the culture I'm immersed in more than what the Bible says? Would I have these same beliefs if I was a Christian brought up in another country or background?

3. Have I ever felt tension between my faith and what I've seen in Christian culture?
   - Are there aspects of American Christianity that feel at odds with who Jesus is?
   - Have I ever witnessed or experienced church hurt, legalism, or hypocrisy?
   - How have I navigated that tension? Did I push it down, walk away, or seek to understand it more deeply?

4. How do I see God working in my life today—not just in the past?
   - Do I have personal experiences that confirm my faith, or do I feel disconnected?
   - Have I taken the time to look for God in the everyday moments, or do I expect to find him only in big, dramatic experiences?
   - When was the last time I felt his presence, his peace, or his guidance?

5. If I stripped away everything I was taught about being a "good Christian," what would my faith look like?
   - If faith isn't about rules or appearances, what *is* it about?
   - Am I more focused on looking like a Christian than actually *being* like Jesus?

- What parts of my faith feel performative, and what parts feel deeply personal and real?

These questions aren't about breaking faith apart just for the sake of questioning—they're about *rebuilding it* on something *real*, *true*, and *personal*. Because when we do the work of figuring out what we *actually* believe—beyond expectations, beyond religious culture, beyond inherited faith—we find something deeper.

We find *Jesus himself*.

FINDING JESUS

It was uncomfortable, a little messy, and, at times, downright disorienting—kind of like realizing that your childhood favorite TV show was actually *terrible*, but you just didn't notice because you were five. But in the middle of all the questioning, I found something deeper than a list of dos and don'ts.

I found *Jesus*—not just the version I had been taught, but the real, raw, unbelievably gracious Jesus who wasn't afraid of my doubts, my struggles, or my side-eye-worthy prayers.

If you've ever felt like you're standing in the middle of a faith crisis, unsure of what's real and what's just religious culture—welcome. You're not alone, and you're definitely not crazy. Let's dive in, ask the hard questions, and figure out what it *really* means to have an identity that's built on Christ—not just on what we were told growing up.

And if at any point this book has made you uncomfortable? Just know, I was probably uncomfortable writing it too. But maybe that's exactly where we need to start.

CONCLUSION

Let Your Light Shine

IF YOU'VE MADE IT THIS FAR, FIRST OF ALL—*look at you!* You've wrestled with questions, sat in the discomfort of doubt, and maybe even torn down some walls you didn't realize were blocking your view of Jesus. And yet here you are, still searching, still seeking, still holding on to faith, even if it looks different from how it looked before.

Now, I don't know about you, but when I first started unraveling parts of my faith, I had this lingering fear that if I let myself ask *too many* questions, if I dug *too deep*, my faith would crumble and I'd be left with nothing. But what have I learned? When something is real, it can handle the weight of your questions. And when you start shedding the stuff that was never meant to be there in the first place—the legalism, the expectations, the performative "good

Christian" act—what's left isn't *less* faith. It's *truer* faith. It's *brighter*. It's *stronger*.

And now? It's time to *live it out*.

Jesus didn't call us to have a faith that sits quietly in the corner, nodding politely, and avoiding hard conversations. He called us to be *a light*—one that shines boldly, bravely, and without fear. But let's be honest: That kind of light can make people uncomfortable, especially the ones who prefer you just go along with everything and don't ask too many questions.

But here's the thing: Faith that is silent, safe, and stagnant was never the goal.

Jesus didn't tell us to dim our light to make others more comfortable. He didn't tell us to blend in, keep quiet, and play nice. He told us to *shine*. To stand out. To bring truth, love, and justice into the world—not just for our own peace of mind, but for the people who desperately need to see a faith that actually looks like Jesus.

I want you to ask yourself:

- What parts of my faith am I still holding back out of fear?
- Where am I feeling called to step up and speak out?
- How can I live out a faith that isn't just *believed* but *embodied*?

Because the world doesn't need more quiet Christians who are afraid to ruffle feathers. The world needs people who have been through the fire, wrestled with the tough stuff, and come out on the other side freer, more rooted, and more on fire than ever before.

Let's stop treating faith like a delicate candle that needs to be protected from the wind.

It was always meant to be a wildfire.

FEELING THE HEAT

One of my favorite stories in the Bible comes from Daniel 3 about three guys named Shadrach, Meshach, and Abednego. If there was ever a group of people who understood what it meant to stand boldly in faith—*and* face the heat for it—it was Shadrach, Meshach, and Abednego.

Their story is one of those Sunday school classics, usually paired with flannel-board figures or a VeggieTales retelling—I prefer the VeggieTales version. But if you strip away the childhood familiarity and really *sit* with it, you'll realize—it's *wild*.

Here's the scene: Three young men, living in exile, faithful to God in a culture that had no interest in their convictions. King Nebuchadnezzar, who had a bit of an ego problem, to put it lightly, built a *massive* golden statue and issued a decree: *Everyone must bow down and worship it—or else.*

No exceptions. No compromises. Just *bow or burn.*

Now, most people—understanding the assignment—took the easy route. They bowed. They didn't necessarily *believe* in the idol, but hey, what's a little kneeling if it saves you from a fiery furnace?

But not Shadrach, Meshach, and Abednego.

They knew the cost. They knew exactly what was at stake. But when given the chance to *save themselves* by bowing, they stood tall.

Their response to the king?

"We do not need to defend ourselves before you in this matter. If we are thrown into the blazing furnace, the God we serve is able to deliver us from it. . . . But even if he does not, we want you to know, Your Majesty, that we will not serve your gods or worship the image of gold you have set up" (Daniel 3:16–18).

Let's pause there for a second, because that's some *next-level* faith.

They weren't just saying, "God will rescue us, so we're not worried." They were saying, "We believe God can rescue us, but *even if he doesn't*, we still won't bow."

That's bold faith. That's *fireproof faith.*

Of course, King Nebuchadnezzar, not known for

handling rejection well, *lost it.* He ordered the furnace heated *seven times hotter,* as if regular fire wasn't bad enough, and had them bound and thrown in.

But here's where the story shifts. Because the moment the king looked into the fire expecting to see three men burning . . . he saw *four.*

"'Weren't there three men that we tied up and threw into the fire?'" he asked. "'Look! I see four men walking around in the fire, unbound and unharmed, and the fourth looks like a son of the gods'" (Daniel 3:24–25).

God didn't *rescue* them before they were thrown in. He didn't *prevent* them from facing the flames.

He met them in the fire.

And when they walked out—because yes, they *walked out*—Scripture says they weren't burned, their clothes weren't scorched, and they didn't even smell like smoke (Daniel 3:27).

THE SAME GOD IN OUR FIRE

This story isn't just about three guys in Babylon. It's about all of us who have ever stood in the tension of faith and fear, of obedience and opposition.

It's about every time we're faced with a choice:

- Stand firm in our faith, even when it costs us something.
- Speak up, even when it makes people uncomfortable.
- Trust God, even when there's no guarantee of the outcome we want.

And it's a reminder that when we make the choice to stand boldly for truth—God stands with us. We don't have to fear the fire, because we are never in it alone.

We might feel the heat of rejection, pushback, or even outright suffering, but God does his best work in the fire. It's in the fire that our faith is refined, our convictions are solidified, and the watching world sees who we really belong to.

The truth is, God never promised to keep us out of the fire. But he *did* promise to be in it with us. So, like Shadrach, Meshach, and Abednego, may we be people who stand tall, even when the world tells us to bow. May we be bold in our faith, even when it costs us something.

And may we remember that our God is not just a rescuer—he's a God who walks in the fire with us.

YOUR SPARK

That spark—the one that flickered in you as a child, the one that made you believe in something bigger than yourself, the one that first whispered to your heart that *there is more*—it's still there.

Maybe it feels dim after years of wrestling with questions and doubts. Maybe it's been buried under expectations, disappointments, or the weight of a faith that started to feel more like an obligation than a relationship. Maybe the world—or even Christian culture itself—has tried to *poof it out*, telling you that curiosity is dangerous, that asking too many questions is a sign of weak faith, that doubt is something to fear instead of something to walk through.

But here's the truth: That spark was never meant to be snuffed out. It was meant to be tended, fed, and fanned into something brighter.

Jesus never called us to a faith that stays quiet, safe, and easily contained. He called us to be a *light*—a fire that cannot be hidden, a flame that illuminates the darkness, a beacon that draws people toward hope. But in order to shine, we have to *embrace* that fire. We have to *harness it, nurture it, and refuse to let fear or complacency dull it.*

That means *leaning in to curiosity instead of suppressing it*—asking the hard questions, searching for real truth, and trusting that God is big enough to handle our doubts.

That means *breaking free from a faith that is just performance*—letting go of the pressure to fit a mold and instead stepping into an identity rooted in *real* relationship with Christ.

That means living boldly, not just believing quietly: refusing to blend in, refusing to dim our faith to make others comfortable, and standing firm even when the world pushes back.

Because when we let our light shine—fully, freely, and without apology—it does more than just illuminate our own path. It brings hope to others. It reminds people who have given up that faith can be real, that Jesus is still moving, that there is space for them here too.

Don't let the world—or even the church—tell you to shrink back.

Don't let anyone convince you that your fire is too much or that your questions disqualify you.

That spark is still in you.

Tend it. Feed it. Let it grow.

Because the world *desperately* needs your light.

ACKNOWLEDGMENTS

I'LL BE THE FIRST TO ADMIT THAT WHEN I stepped into this publishing process, I had no idea what I was doing. The dream had lived in my heart for nearly twenty years, but dreaming and doing are two very different things. I had stories and ideas—plenty of words—but gathering them together under a message I cared so deeply about became both a difficult and divine process.

People warned me that writing a book would force me to test the very truths I was trying to share. I nodded politely, thinking I understood. I didn't. Not really. Not until life asked me to live every word I was wrestling onto the page.

J deployed just two days before my manuscript was due. Suddenly, I found myself sitting inside the very "holy soul friction" I was trying to write about. I was living the dream of becoming an author while solo parenting, grieving another year marked by infertility, and asking God to meet me in the tension of joy and longing all over again.

There is no way I would have made it to the finish line with this book if it weren't for an incredible team of people professionally and supportive villagers privately who walked with me through the holy chaos of writing it. Thank you for believing in me, cheering me on, and holding space for the stories that shaped these pages. With that being said, there are a few people I would like to thank.

To my literary agent, Kathleen Kerr, I will never forget almost deleting your email in the parking lot of Home Goods in Kansas City because I thought it was spam. In a difficult season, it seemed too good to be true. Your belief in me, my story, and convictions has been redemptive and healing in a way I truly didn't know how to pray for.

To my editor, Brigitta Nortker, working with you and Thomas Nelson has been nothing but a dream come true. There are few people in this world that make me feel as seen and validated as you do. Your ability to know when I needed encouragement, a listening ear, and extra nudge made this process possible.

Kathleen and Brigitta, thank you for holding my hand, answering endless questions, for all the patience, and being such strong advocates. I admire you both so much.

To Kristen Golden, Devin Duke, Janene MacIvor, and

everyone at Thomas Nelson, thank you for holding my words with care and helping me tell this story with honesty and hope. Your talents and professionalism have been a gift to me, thank you!

To Dr. Faithe Beam, the first person I shared the dream of being a Christian writer with between two leather seats at Creek Coffee House, well over a decade ago. When I told you where I saw God leading me, you never made me feel crazy or like it was improbable like others. You simply said, "I see that for you too," and I have held on to those words ever since. Years later, it was with you on that Pilgrimage to Cape Town in 2017 that "Soul Friction" first started stirring in my spirit, and hence the idea for this book was born. Thank you for being there in my desperate hours and greatest achievements, I hope you know the ripple effect of your life and ministry go far beyond "the creek."

To my Benson Baptist Church family, you have always been my grounding place and sanctuary. Thank you for letting me wrestle with the questions out loud and for being a living example of the faith and community I write about here.

To my parents, I hope the way I told these stories makes you proud. Thank you for showing me what it looks like to cling to faith and hold fast to Jesus. You were the phone call after every dark moment and the first clap after every win. You helped pick up the pieces each time and reminded me that God was still holding me in the palm of His hand. I pray I serve God and His people with the same steadfastness and compassion you've modeled my whole life.

Mom, your daily devotion and reverence for the Word are the reason I fell in love with Scripture. Thank you for loving me unconditionally and for your patience when I asked a hundred questions or wanted to wrestle through an idea. Your faith shaped me in ways I'm still discovering. I wouldn't be who I am—or writing this book—without you.

Dad, those hours in the darkroom, singing "This Little Light of Mine" and "You Are My Sunshine," planted more than just melodies in my heart. Watching you use your creativity as part of your calling showed me that God doesn't waste our gifts—He uses them. Your example gave me the confidence to pursue this work with courage and joy.

Mama Dorothy, your prayers have carried me around the world and back. Your love of God and family has been the glue that holds our family together, thank you for being the epitome of a strong southern woman.

To my Papa, I've heard words "There's my baby doll . . . oh,.she can handle it!" in the late hours of writing and dark moments of self-doubt. Though you are not physically here, I know you have been with me every step of this journey. I am so grateful for the tenacity, hustle, and passion you instilled in me all those years ago.

To my friends and family who sent texts when you knew I wasn't sleeping, bought coffee when I was running on fumes, and prayed when I ran out of words. Thank you for always reminding me that I am not alone, I truly have the best village.

To Zadie Ann, I pray that when you're old enough to read this book, it simply echoes everything I've been whispering to you your whole life. It is good to ask big questions. It's okay to not have every answer. And it's more than okay to change your mind as you grow.

God is for you, He is with you, and He loves you more deeply than you can imagine. Being your momma is the greatest joy and honor of my life. Keep letting your light shine, sweet girl—the world is brighter because you're in it.

To J, my steady in every season—thank you for holding space for this dream long before it had words. Thank you for listening to every wild idea, answering every "quick question," and never once making me feel like I was too much. You are the safe place where I can unmask and simply be myself.

You have never dimmed my fire—not when it burned bright, not when it flickered, not when it felt like too much for me to carry. Instead, you've stood beside me, held me up, and reminded me who I am when I forget.

I am inspired daily by your strength, your discipline, and the quiet, steady way you lead our family. You make me braver, softer, and better in all the ways that matter. Thank you for loving me in a way that makes this work possible.

And finally, to the women reading this book, especially the ones who have felt shame, silence, or smallness —you are the reason I wrote it. I pray these words remind you that you were never too much, never too far gone, and never too late to begin again.

This book was never just mine—it was ours. A little holy, a little chaotic, and held together by grace.

ABOUT THE AUTHOR

IN 2016, KENDALL FOUNDED UNAPOLOGETIC Ministry, a blog and community focused on topics that are often taboo in church—infertility, depression, anxiety, and eating disorders, just to name a few. Kendall and her husband, Justin, live in their hometown of Benson, North Carolina, where she loves to share a glimpse into their small-town life.